Heartstrings
A Biography of Wilmos Csehy

Heartstrings
A Biography of Wilmos Csehy
1914-1983

by Barbara M. Sutryn

*"He makes the violin sing the song that
his soul must be singing."*
—Music Critic
Toronto Telegram

LAMP POST PUBLISHING, INC.
Montoursville, Pennsylvania

© 2004 Barbara M. Sutryn
Illustrations © 2004 Ellen Black
Cover Design © 2004 Lamp Post Publishing, Inc.

All rights reserved. No part of this book may be reproduced or transmitted in any form or means, electronic or mechanical, including photocopying, recording, or any information storage and retrieval system, without written permission from the author, except for the inclusion of brief quotations in a review.

First Edition 2004
ISBN 1-892135-33-7
Library of Congress Control Number: 2004105050

Lamp Post Publishing, Inc.
1741 Tallman Hollow Road
Montoursville, PA 17754
www.HeartstringsBio.com

Printed in the United States of America on acid-free paper

Acknowledgements

to Gladys Csehy who provided much
of the material included in this book,

and to Wilmos Csehy's many friends
and associates who graciously shared their memories.

Three deserve special mention:

Adi Cierpke

Rev. Wesley White

Dr. Ronald Alan Matthews
who loaned the transcript of a 1983 interview with
Mr. Csehy, portions of which appeared in PCB
Magazine,
Fall-Winter 1990-1991

Photographs used by permission of
Gladys Csehy,
Adi Cierpke,
Molly Fung Dumm,
Philip H. C. Fung,
Dr. Gordon Bobett,
and
The Csehy Summer School of Music

Sketches used by permission of the artist:
Ellen Black.

Shown on the cover is the Carlo Ferdinando Landolfi violin that belonged to Wilmos Csehy. (Photographed by Philip H. C. Fung.)

The cover background was photographed by Kendra Billman at J. R. Judd Violins in Williamsport, Pennsylvania.

*"He took my life into his life
and prayed for my growth and improvement."*
—Samuel Hsu

Wilmos Csehy
1914-1983

*"In seminary I came across a saying of Sophocles,
'Wise men weep easily.'
I always thought of Wilmos Csehy
as the example of this."*
—Wesley White

*Christians should strive
for excellence.*
—Wilmos Csehy

Chapter 1

On a hot summer day, campers arrived at Muncy Terraces carrying suitcases, duffel bags, and bulky instruments—trumpets, French horns, violins, even drums.

"Hey! You're back!" they shouted happily to old friends.

Wesley White, sixteen, sullenly lugged his trombone over into the shade of a towering old pine tree, apart from these happy reunions. He was not part of them and didn't want to be.

"If I make it through this month, I'll never come back again," he muttered to himself. He was here only because his parents and grandparents had ganged up on him. When they registered him for the Csehy Summer School of Music, they overrode his own plans for the summer. He was fed up with his friends asking, "The *What* School? Where's that?"

"Halfway to nowhere," he would answer. From his home in Michigan, that's where Pennsylvania seemed to be.

He put on his most bored expression now when he was being welcomed by "Uncle Wilmos" and "Aunt Gladys," and only half-listened to them explain their impossible last name. "Csehy, is Hungarian," they said. They pronounced the Cse- like the *che* in chess. *Cheh'-he*.

Wes waited for them to make some remark about his shoulder-length hair. Surely they would refuse to let him in, and he could get back in the car and go home—or to Interlochen Music Camp in Michigan, where his friends from the school band were going. If they wouldn't accept him here, he would be off the hook!

Wes thought nothing could be better than life in Detroit. He had been born in Zaire where his father served as a missionary doctor. The previous year the family had relocated to Michigan. What wonderful new opportunities there were in the United States! He was happy, but his parents seemed to disapprove of everything he and his brother did.

The boys were in high school now; naturally they were trying new things. But Wes often saw his parents shaking their heads. "There's danger in the things teenagers are doing—the casual use of drugs, experiments with sex, and worse…," they would say.

The two boys insisted on dressing like their new friends. Wes could ignore his mother's comments about his clothes, but when his parents discovered their sons were starting to use drugs, and warned them of the danger, he rebelled.

Wes knew perfectly well why he had been sent to the Csehy School. His mother and dad hoped that a month in the Christian atmosphere here would change his attitude.

He ventured a look at Mr. Csehy's face. The welcoming smile had not faded. Could it be that there was no dress code here? He had deliberately worn the ragged jeans that made his mother cringe. So far no one had mentioned them.

But almost as though they could read his thoughts, someone asked, "Did you bring your concert clothes?"

"Of course," he answered crossly. He'd brought his suit and tie, along with everything else on the camp list. He knew from the brochure that each Saturday night the students and faculty would put on a concert for the public. He'd done enough singing and trombone playing in churches at home to know how to dress properly for performances.

He sighed. The only way to survive a month here would be to concentrate on the music part and steer clear of the religion. He glanced around, wondering who would be the first to pounce on him with a sermon.

"This is my first year. You, too?" asked a girl he had seen when he first arrived.

"Yeah," he said. He had no desire to talk to her. But, suddenly he remembered something. "You aren't new. I heard them call you by name when you went up to register."

"Isn't that something!" She sounded amazed and delighted. "Imagine knowing me just from the picture I sent with my registration!"

What were these Csehy people really like? Wes began to wonder. He said little to the other campers, but kept his eye on the director.

"Uncle Wilmos" Csehy chatted with the campers as they went in to the manor house for dinner. He asked one of the younger boys, "Did you get that big heavy suitcase down to the dorm all right?"

When they were all settled at the tables, he had them sing together before he asked God's blessing on the meal. The way he spoke reminded Wes a little of his own grandfather.

From his place at the dinner table, Wes looked through the windows at the mountains and the tall evergreens that created cool, shady spots on the campus. The smell of pine had stayed on his hands. There should be great places here to get away by myself, he thought.

"See you all at Sing Time," Uncle Wilmos told them as they left the dining room.

"'Sing Time'? What a corny name!" a new camper muttered.

And corny music, Wes thought, when he heard them begin to sing a chorus he'd known all his life,

"I've got a home in glory land that outshines the sun…"

When they had sung the last line, Uncle Wilmos explained that the song was one the southern blacks might have sung to console themselves as they slaved in the cotton fields under a blistering hot sun. Heaven was their only hope. "Sing it for me again, that way."

The voices of campers and counselors and teachers joined in singing it slowly this time, as it might have been sung by the slaves. Wes could tell by the faces around him, that he was not the only one who found this an emotional experience.

When Wilmos Csehy picked up his violin, his wife, Gladys, took her seat at the piano. Wes marveled at these skilled musicians playing together as though they were one person. Many of the things they played were their own arrangements of familiar hymns, but no matter what they chose, the campers were drawn into the music that seemed to come straight from their hearts.

"Sing Time is the best time of the day," new campers were writing home.

Wes found his days filled with trombone practice, private lessons, and rehearsals for band, orchestra or chorus. He almost forgot that he didn't want to be here, reveling in this glut of music. And he was surprised to find himself looking forward to Sing Time each evening.

Heartstrings

Tuesday morning, just before his private lesson was no time for his trombone to act up! It wasn't holding the pitch right. He was there in the patch of pine grove he had chosen for his practice spot, looking at the instrument in annoyance. *How can I get this to a repair shop?* he was wondering, when Uncle Wilmos walked by.

"How's it going, Wes?"

"It's not going. I don't think I can play with the orchestra unless I can get my trombone fixed."

"Oh? What's wrong?"

"I don't know. It keeps going flat. Do you know any place I can take it to be repaired?"

"Let's take a look at it." Wes watched as the musician turned it around in his hands, examining it. "I think I know what's wrong. Come on over to my shop with me."

Astonished that Uncle Wilmos would take time to repair his trombone—astonished that he might be *able* to repair his trombone—Wes followed him across the campus to Ye Olde Fiddle Shoppe.

It was the first time he had been in the violin studio. On one wall were pictures of Wilmos Csehy and his father. There was a collection of instruments—old violins, a cello, a baritone horn, and a euphonium hanging off by itself in one corner; there were dozens of bows; there were violins in many sizes; there were violins that had been taken apart for repair. Catalogs galore cluttered the small shop.

But Wilmos knew exactly where to reach for a cork to fix a trombone. "There that should do it," he said, handing it back to Wes. His smile seemed to say he enjoyed being able to help. "Give it a try."

Wes wondered how a man whose head was so full of the knowledge of violins could have room in his brain to understand trombones as well.

He was beginning to think there was no end to what this man knew. Often, in the dining room, Uncle Wilmos would pass on tips that were helpful to young musicians. Anything from how to live through an on-stage mistake to being accompanied by an out-of-tune piano. "Now you'll have applause to deal with," he told them one day, and proceeded to demonstrate just how a professional should bow in acknowledgment. It was one of the tidbits Wes stored away to use back home.

Interior view of Ye Olde Fiddle Shoppe at Muncy Terraces. 1970s

Heartstrings

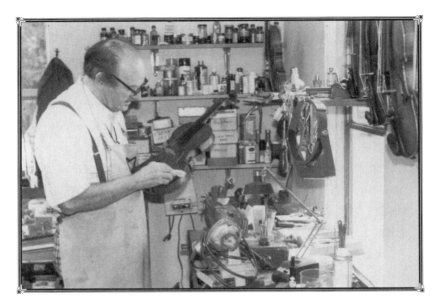

Wilmos Csehy working on a violin in Ye Olde Fiddle Shoppe at Muncy Terraces.

A few of his dorm mates who were on their track teams at school got up early each morning to run. Wes was not a dedicated runner, but he usually got up at the same time and started out with them. Soon he would be left behind, running alone. Sometimes he would pass Uncle Wilmos walking along, looking at some kind of list. He, too, was an early riser. Back in the dorm, he mentioned these early-morning encounters.

"Oh, don't you know what he was doing?" his counselor asked, when Wes mentioned it to him. "He was praying. He carries a list of students with him, to be sure he prays for each one."

"He prays for me?" Wes wasn't sure that was good. Next would come the preaching.

"He prays for us, too—thank goodness!" the counselor said.

Wes watched the heavy-set, grandpa-like camp director walking around the grounds, conspicuous in the wild, colorful shirts he wore. Often, he would see him put his arm around a camper or instructor he overtook on his path, then walk a ways with him, talking as they walked. He wondered what that would be like.

When Wes felt that arm around *his* shoulders one day, he knew positively that he was important to this great and gentle musician.

He tried to remind himself that this music camp wasn't anything special, and it hadn't been his idea to come here. But he couldn't help being impressed with the musical skills of the Csehys and the other teachers. It was amazing to him that they were all genuinely devoted to helping the students develop their talents.

But he was even more impressed with the depth of their Christian faith.

Suddenly—too soon—camp was over and his father was there to pick him up. Wes had always been able to talk to his dad, even during the last rough year when he and his parents had disagreed so often.

They stood together now on one of the top tiers of the terrace, looking out at the mountains, with the band shell in the foreground. In a few hours Dr. White would be sitting on that terrace with the audience, listening to the outdoor concert; Wes would be seated on the stage they were facing, playing his trombone.

It was time to talk.

Wes admitted to being confused about a lot of things. Finally he blurted out, "Dad, I just know God is real and out there somewhere." He told his father he would be searching—needing to find God for himself.

By the spring of that year he had found God and accepted Christ as his Savior. That decision changed the direction of his life.

When he went back to camp the next summer, he wasn't worried about being rejected because of his clothes or hairstyle or anything else. Uncle Wilmos loved him. Uncle Wilmos would welcome him just as he was.

That second year Wes began to soak up the words of the older man—those he heard in private, and those he heard in chapel or Sing Time. "Christ is your Shepherd to lead and direct you and take you to green pastures," he would say. Or when settling a dispute between campers, "We need to talk to our Father about this." It pleased Wes that Uncle Wilmos sometimes came looking for him, just to talk.

This year Wes was to be on one of the student teams that went out from camp on Sundays to play for nearby church services. He was looking forward to it. On Saturday as he walked across campus, he felt the familiar arm around the shoulder, then heard a gentle suggestion.

"Now Wes, you're going to be on a team representing the school. Wouldn't you like to make Uncle Wilmos happy and just get a little cut off your hair?"

As though this were a great new idea that had never been suggested to him before, he was off to town like a shot. He was surprised to hear himself say to the barber, "Cut it as short as you can."

Wes came to love the atmosphere at Csehy. The combination of music and Christian love drew him back year after year—four times as a student, then as a counselor, and eventually as the instructor in low brass instruments.

As an adult he became a close personal friend of Wilmos Csehy, and they shared their dreams for the school. He learned that this man he so admired served God not only through public concerts and teaching, but in quiet, humble ways that few people would ever know about.

He gradually learned the story of his life—the experiences that produced a man who made people, both students and adults, feel they knew God better when they had spent time with him. He began to understand why this accomplished violinist had traded the fame of the concert stage for "Sing Time" at a summer camp.

His violin style had the flavor of his Hungarian background.
—Molly Fung

Chapter 2

When Wilmos' father, Michael Csehy, came to America from Hungary in the early 1900s he did not bring much with him. He did not have much to bring. But he carried—ever so carefully—his precious violin.

Coming as a young man looking for a new life, he did not immediately settle in New York City, as many of the European immigrants did. After wandering around for a while to see the country, he settled about sixty miles west of New York in the small town of Flemington, New Jersey.

The established Hungarian community in Flemington made him feel right at home. By the time he met Elizabeth, also from Hungary, and persuaded her to be his wife, he and his violin playing were fairly well known. Music was the most important part of his life, and he was teaching several students as well as performing, but he supported himself by working at other jobs by day,

Heartstrings

eventually becoming a glass cutter at the Flemington Glass Company.

Things did not start out well for the young Michael and Elizabeth Csehy. Their first son died shortly after birth, and a baby daughter lived only a little while. Then their third child died. None lived beyond the age of five.

So Wilmos, born February 10, 1914, was especially precious to them.

"How wonderful to have a boy who will play beautiful music with me," Michael said to his wife.

"Already you are thinking of a violin for him, before he is even big enough to hold his rattle!" Elizabeth laughed.

Although they could understand and speak enough English to get by in their adopted country, they spoke to each other in Hungarian. That was the language in which Wilmos would learn to say his first words.

They enjoyed the old customs. Playing familiar Hungarian music was one way of remembering home.

The father watched little Wilmos and patiently waited. One day, before the boy's third birthday, he said, "Here, son, I have something for you," and put a small violin in his hands.

It was a tiny metal instrument Michael had fixed up especially for him. At first his father taught him, just about the violin. Then, after a few months, he let him play a few notes, using only open strings. For a long time the child didn't even realize he would need to use his fingers to play as his father did.

Wilmos Csehy, age 4-5. Wilmos is frowning because the photographer had insisted, for an earlier shot, that he pose with the violin in the wrong hand

Heartstrings

It was just the right gift at the right time. About a year later he received a good 1/8 size violin. On that instrument, Wilmos Csehy gave his first concert. He was four and a half years old when he was lifted up to stand on a grand piano and play before an audience.

His father was an excellent teacher, knowing just when it was time to start a new lesson. He made music so enjoyable that it became the boy's lifelong passion.

Wilmos' boyhood was quite different from that of a small boy today or even most boys of that day. The Hungarian folks in Flemington kept apart from the other people in town. They had their own social hall where they gathered. Some of them helped to establish a Catholic Church there, but others traveled to New Brunswick where there was an Hungarian Reformed Church. Their children were sent to the Hungarian school in New Brunswick.

The Csehys wanted their son to be Hungarian even though he had been born in the United States. Because he grew up speaking his parents' language and absorbed so much of their culture, he was often mistakenly introduced as Hungarian-born. In the restricted community of his early years he learned little about how other people lived.

What he did learn about, however, was music. He was surrounded by it. He listened to his father playing and heard the students' lessons. His father played with an Hungarian gypsy band, and he listened to them rehearsing. There was the music that he made himself.

Wilmos Csehy, on right, playing his violin with some of the members of his father's Hungarian Band. 1920's

And the wonderful concerts! "Will we go to hear Mr. Damrosch's orchestra tonight?" he would ask. He was always eager to go along when his father took a group of his students to the New York Symphony which his friend conducted. Whenever he could, Mr. Csehy, the teacher, gave the young violinists an opportunity to meet and talk with the accomplished musicians who played in the orchestra.

Another night it might be a concert by Fritz Kreisler, who composed so much of his own music. Or a performance by Jascha Heifetz. What a treat it was to hear these outstanding, world-famous violinists.

Wilmos was not so fond of the Psalms sung at home in the tradition of the old country. Mr. Csehy would sing a line of the Psalm without accompaniment, and the others would sing it after him. The Psalms were long. Sometimes Wilmos thought, too long.

"Dad, everyone knows the words; why can't we just sing them without hearing you sing them alone first?" he pleaded. But where tradition was concerned, his father was unbending, and Wilmos often fell asleep before the Psalm was ended.

Wilmos' ability on the violin was soon so well known that, even at a young age, he was performing often. So when other little boys might be outside playing mumblety-peg, he was absorbed in practicing.

In those days it wasn't taken for granted that everyone would go to school for twelve years, and then perhaps continue with college. For Wilmos, as for many children then, schooling was an off-and-on-again thing.

While the regular school schedule included a full day of classes, Wilmos' father arranged for him to go in the morning one day and in the afternoon the next, but sometimes kept him home all day so that he could practice the violin. Even when he went to school, Wilmos would take his fingerboard with him to practice on whenever there was an opportunity.

School was difficult for the boy because he was just beginning to learn English, the language of his teachers and classmates. He had to have his father translate the assignments so he could do them. So, although the focus of his training was on music and his schooling was irregular, he managed to learn the standard subjects and other useful skills he would need as he grew up.

His family belonged to the Reformed Church of Hungary, but they—especially his grandmother—felt-there was something missing in their religious understanding.

An evangelist from the Trenton area came to Flemington, and went from one house to another distributing booklets in the Hungarian neighborhood. The Csehys decided to visit his meetings.

"What is he saying?" Wilmos would ask his mother, as they sat in the service. He had not been among English-speaking people enough to be able to understand the preacher's words. His mother would try to explain, but she herself could not always grasp the exact meaning.

When those services ended, Sunday afternoon meetings were started, and Wilmos was asked to play for them. He was ten years old and did not know much about what was going on. He wished he could understand the English words better. He was curious about what the preacher was saying.

Toward the end of each service, he would see people coming to the front of the auditorium. He wasn't sure why they were coming, but thought it was because they were going to get something free. One night he, too, went to the altar.

His mother joined him there to act as interpreter. Although she herself had not been clear about what was offered, she understood enough English for the preacher to be able to explain to her, and she could relay the information to her son. Both Wilmos and his mother learned that night that Jesus Christ had died to be their personal Savior, and they accepted His gift of salvation.

At first, his father thought it was a foolish thing to do—something they would get over. But it wasn't long before he, too, accepted Christ.

Wilmos thought surely now they would begin to sing the hymns at home that he heard in church, but his father stuck with the old familiar way of singing the Psalms.

If anyone had asked Wilmos what he wanted to be when he grew up, he would have been puzzled. He was a violinist. He would always be a violinist. How could he be anything else?

It came as a surprise to him, when he was twelve years old, to learn from someone outside his home that he had been adopted. But he felt such a close bond with his family that he never showed any interest in trying to identify his birth parents. He was satisfied with whatever they chose to tell him about his parentage.

Later attempts by others to verify this through court records were unsuccessful, as adoption proceedings in those days changed the birth record of the child to name the adopting parents in place of the natural parents. They were a family. That was enough for Wilmos.

Wilmos Csehy and his father, Michael Csehy, playing their violins together at their home in Flemington, New Jersey. Probably early 1940's

Heartstrings

His father encouraged his musical ambitions and was pleased that he was often asked to perform in church and other places.

But the time came when Michael could no longer teach his son. Wilmos had gone beyond him in his skill at playing the violin.

"I want to study with a great violinist," Wilmos told his father. "I want to study with Leopold Auer! He has taught Jascha Heifetz and Mischa Elman and Efrem Zimbalist. I want to be able to play as they can play!"

Surely the great violin teacher could help him to reach new heights, they agreed.

But it was not to be. Mr. Auer looked at the teenager and said, "No, I'm sorry. You are still too young to be my student. You must wait a little."

Wilmos could not wait. He persuaded Mr. Auer's assistant, Albert Stretch, to take him on and began his lessons with him.

By now invitations were coming from every direction for him to give concert performances and to play with this group or that. One invitation offered him the position of violin soloist with a symphony orchestra in New Jersey. He was leaning toward acceptance when his mother heard that Dr. Leon Tucker was coming to a town not far from Flemington. He was known as an evangelist, but she had heard that he was also a great Bible teacher.

"I think we should go to hear him," she told the family.

Wilmos had no desire to go. He looked at the notice again. "Dr. Leon Tucker and the Musical Messengers," he read. "I wonder what kind of music they will have."

Once there, it was Dr. Tucker's message that reached his heart. He gave his life and his music to the Lord that night.

Someone had told Dr. Tucker that Wilmos was an excellent violinist and a few weeks after that service, Wilmos got a letter asking him to join Dr. Tucker's Musical Messengers.

He found himself faced with the most difficult choice he had ever had to make.

Which offer should he accept—the one from Dr. Tucker, or the one from the orchestra? From the financial standpoint, the orchestra would certainly be the better choice. But he wanted to serve the Lord with his music, and, while he wouldn't earn much money playing for Dr. Tucker's meetings, it would be a foot in the door. When he was better known, he might be asked to play for "big name" evangelists. He mistakenly thought that would be a lucrative career.

When he asked his mother's advice, she told him to pray about it before deciding.

Wilmos went to his room and got down on his knees, with one of the letters in each hand. He prayed. He struggled. He wept. When he finally got to his feet, the letter from Dr. Tucker looked just as it had before. The one from the orchestra had been crumpled into a ball.

He took that to be God's way of saying, "Yes, I really do want you to serve me with your music. I want you to go with Dr. Tucker."

So it was decided. He joined Dr. Tucker, only to discover that things were not exactly as he had imagined them. It was humbling to receive his first week's pay—$11. Dr. Tucker was adamant about tithing, insisting that Wilmos contribute a tenth of his pay. This so disgusted Wilmos that he gave back the entire amount.

But Wilmos' outlook changed greatly as he sat under Dr. Tucker's preaching night after night. He underwent a great spiritual growth spurt. He began to see his talent as something he could give back to God, and he realized that this was not likely to be financially rewarding.

He came to believe firmly that he had been called to do the Lord's work through music, just as a pastor is called to do his work through preaching. He was sure that God had plans for him.

That was a concept his musician friends did not understand. Wilmos turned down an invitation to play with Fred Waring's "Pennsylvanians." He refused an offer from the New York Philharmonic Orchestra.

He explained that he would be glad to play with them if it would fit into his program. But since he could not take on that sort of commitment and give priority to the work that was all-important to him, he refused the offers.

Starting out on the road with Dr. Tucker began nearly fifty years of traveling back and forth across the country to take his music where he believed God wanted to use it.

It's a gift the Lord has given me.
—Wilmos Csehy

Chapter 3

For a year, Wilmos Csehy traveled with Dr. Tucker's Musical Messengers. The musicians in the group would play and sing before Dr. Tucker preached. Wilmos began to recognize the importance of making the music a part of the ministry, not just a musical performance.

For Wilmos, who made it a habit to practice at least four, sometimes six, hours a day, his time was well filled.

Earlier, as a boy of ten, Wilmos had shown an unusually deep interest in knowing God. In his teens when he responded to Dr. Tucker's preaching, it was to make a gift of his violin playing to the Lord.

After he had been on the road with Dr. Tucker for about a year he began to reconsider the direction this was taking him.

He told himself that there was certainly more than one way he could serve the Lord with his music, and he began to look at the options. "Instead of staying with this particular group, maybe I should strike out on my own."

Heartstrings

He had never felt there was anything wrong in playing with a secular group. The offer was still open for him to go back to Flemington and play with the orchestra. He thought if he did that he would still have plenty of opportunities to give concerts of sacred music.

There may have been financial reasons for this debate with himself. Perhaps he thought it was time to begin earning the kind of money the secular world offered. He was still receiving only eleven dollars a week from Dr. Tucker. But he knew that by making such a move, he would be giving sacred music second place.

He struggled, as he had before, over the choice between a secular career and obedience to the call he felt to serve the Lord. Finally he told Dr. Tucker that he would be leaving.

But the evangelist asked him to stay with the group just a little bit longer—at least through the meetings scheduled to start the following week in Franklin, Pennsylvania.

At the Tabernacle in Franklin, before the evening meeting began, Dr. Tucker called Wilmos aside. "I want you to do something for me." He nodded toward one of the two pianos. "I want you to go over and stand near that piano. There's a young lady here who wants to come with us as a Musical Messenger. I told her she could play along with the hymns tonight.

"She's there now. You just get over there where you can hear her and let me know what you think."

What Wilmos thought, when he heard her creative, rippling accompaniment to the singing, was that this girl could PLAY! It was the kind of music, coming from the heart, that matched Wilmos' own.

In a matter of days, Gladys Williamson was part of the Musical Messengers. Dr. Tucker was pleased. Wilmos was more than pleased.

Perhaps it was her music that he noticed at first, but it wasn't long before he was captivated by her beauty and personality.

In fact, the attraction was so strong, he put his return to Flemington on hold. When the team moved on to Clarion, Pennsylvania, Wilmos went with them, keeping an eye on the charming new pianist. He followed them to their next stop, Indiana, Pennsylvania.

When Gladys accompanied him on the violin she had a remarkable way of matching his expression. And to his delight, accompanying him seemed to be her greatest pleasure.

"You could be a concert soloist," he told her.

"But I wouldn't enjoy that," she answered. "I have always preferred to do accompaniment."

Wilmos was expected back in Flemington, but he decided to stay with the group for just one more series of meetings in Meadville, Pennsylvania.

Heartstrings

The more Wilmos and Gladys played together, the more completely they blended, and the more creative they became in combining with the other instruments and voices.

Among the musicians in the group was a girl who played a set of little bells—piccolo cowbells, they called them. They fascinated Wilmos. "Gladys you've got to have a set of bells like those."

Both of them were passionate about music. It was not surprising that this fulfilling partnership in music drew them together emotionally.

Wilmos still planned to return to New Jersey to play with the orchestra, but he couldn't just walk away from the romance that was developing. And Gladys, he knew, intended to continue with the Musical Messengers.

The night she wore her green dress, he simply abandoned the idea of joining the orchestra and asked her to marry him. The next time they played together publicly, she was wearing his engagement ring.

So when he did leave Leon Tucker's Musical Messengers, he left with Gladys. They went to her home in Alliance, Ohio to be married.

In those days a young man was expected to save up some money before he married. He was usually in his late twenties before he could go to the girl's father and assure him that he was able to provide for a wife.

There was no question that Wilmos Csehy would be able to earn a living with his violin. But he was only eighteen! Up to this point he had not been performing where audiences would pay well to hear him. He had played, instead, in churches and evangelistic meetings where the speaker would share with the musicians a bit of the love offerings that were given. The money that came in was always "just enough" to pay their expenses, as they traveled from one engagement to the next. How would Gladys' parents feel about such a hand-to-mouth existence, he wondered.

"I don't think you need to worry about that," Gladys told him. Her family understood that she had given her talents to serve the Lord, and they fully expected God to provide her needs if she was obedient to Him.

"That's exactly the way I feel about it," Wilmos said, relieved.

His family, too, believed that obedience to the Lord's call meant depending on Him for every need. His father willingly signed the consent form for his underage son to marry.

While her parents could trust God to care for His servants, they couldn't help wondering—did these youngsters really know what they were doing? "He's a wonderful, talented young man, Gladys, but you've known him only a couple of months!" her mother said.

But that was just a first-gasp reaction. Her family was quickly won over and the wedding took place in their home two weeks later.

Heartstrings

The Tabernacle in Franklin where they had first seen each other was operated by Mr. and Mrs. L. P. Lehman. The Lehmans also had a large Tabernacle on the island in Wheeling, WV, where evangelistic meetings were held every night of the week, all year long. Their son, Paul, known as Junior Lehman, was eighteen at the time—just Wilmos' age—but was already attracting crowds as "The Boy Preacher."

When the Lehmans learned that Wilmos and Gladys were available, they invited the couple to come to Wheeling to be on the staff. The newlyweds saw this as immediate confirmation that the Lord would provide for them.

Once Wilmos had turned down the position with the orchestra, he never again considered leaving full-time Christian work. They left for Wheeling just two days after they were married, to begin their work with the Lehmans in the large 6,000-seat Tabernacle.

There they were broadcasting fourteen hours a week, and went out almost every night to give musical programs in other towns. It was satisfying work for them, in a way that they knew secular work could never be.

One of the first things the newly married couple did was order a set of bells from a man they had found in Hartford, Connecticut, who made them. They purchased twenty-seven, enough for two octaves—paying one dollar for each bell.

During their time with the Lehmans they shared the platform at the two Lehman Tabernacles with Billy Sunday and other well-known evangelists. They were there just eight months, when they felt they needed to leave and go back to Gladys' home in Ohio.

Again, the Lord was showing that he knew their needs and had already prepared for them. They were expecting their first baby, when Gladys became seriously ill with a kidney infection and had to be taken to the hospital.

Even there, recovery was slow. There were no miracle drugs. It was three weeks before she could leave the hospital to return to her parents' home.

There, with good care, she regained her strength and had her first child, a daughter whom they named Wilma Jean.

While he was with Dr. Tucker, Wilmos had begun playing a trumpet, and soon after they were married he took up the French horn. He and Gladys had mastered the bells. Adding these to the violin and piano they could now offer a much more varied musical package. They decided to travel on their own, as a couple, continuing to do the same sort of musical concerts they had done before.

But now they would have a baby traveling with them.

Preparing for their first tour made busy days for the new mother. They were not yet widely known beyond their home area, so the first order of business was to find places where their ministry would be welcomed.

Gladys took on the job of arranging the bookings, making sure that they allowed time to travel from the last performance in one town to the first concert in the next. She became an expert with maps, finding the best routes across the states.

By the time Wilma Jean was six weeks old, the family was ready to go back on the road.

Many traveling musicians, before agreeing to do a concert, would insist that the host church promise a certain amount of money.

"I don't want to do that," Wilmos said. "I want us to play wherever we can bring honor to God."

Still, they did have to eat. And take care of their little daughter. And buy gas to get from one engagement to the next.

"Our heavenly Father knows our needs," they would remind each other. They would trust God for all things. But they would also do their part by keeping expenses down as much as they could.

One way they could cut costs was by staying in private homes rather than hotels. At each place where they booked a concert they would ask to stay with families from that church.

Most of the time they were playing for evangelistic meetings that ran for two weeks. That gave them time to get acquainted with their hosts and to share their music with other people in the community.

"Would you play for the people out at the old folks' home?" someone would ask. If they could arrange a time, they would do it.

Gladys and Wilmos Csehy. A young couple faced with difficult decisions.

In 1936, after they had been on their own for a year, their son Richard was born, and for a while they traveled with two children.

These were hard times for people all across the country. Many men were out of work; families were losing their homes. It was a no-frills time. The Csehys, who would go wherever God called them, had their faith challenged as they waited day by day, meal by meal, for Him to provide their needs.

Concerts they had arranged were sometimes as far as five hundred miles apart. Not five hundred easy miles on modern interstate highways. In the 1930s, even the main roads were likely to be twisting, hilly, poorly paved two-laners. Pulling a heavy trailer slowed their speed even more.

After traveling with their family and struggling to make ends meet, they listened with an open mind when the evangelist, Dwight Ferguson, invited them to go with him on a one-year tour. It sounded like a wonderful opportunity.

But it had a down side.

"No, we couldn't take the children," Wilmos told Gladys, as they discussed this invitation.

But how could they leave them? They had to remind each other that missionaries were often separated from their children for years at a time. It was one of the sacrifices that was expected of them if they were to follow God's call. It seemed the Csehys were being asked to do the same.

So, difficult as it was, the two babies were left with Gladys' parents in Ohio. Wilma Jean was just turning two; Richard was six months old.

Their thoughts were often back in Ohio, as they zigzagged back and forth across the country, playing in California, Minnesota, Arizona, New Mexico, then up to Chicago and back down to Texas, wherever Rev. Ferguson's speaking engagements took him.

Time out for fishing in Santa Rosa, California, 1934. Left to right Wilmos Csehy, Rev. Ferguson, Rev. Dyke, Mr. Sleipness. Wilmos caught all but two of the fish displayed.

Heartstrings

At one point, they were playing in a little mission church in Arizona, near Tucson. There they saw real poverty among the people. An elderly woman acted as minister of the very primitive church. The offerings, of course, were very small.

All along the way they had used the offerings from one church to get them to the next. They were scheduled to go from this little Arizona mission church to a series of meetings in California.

But when Rev. Ferguson had finished his mission and was ready to move on, there wasn't enough money to buy gas to take them to California. The church where they were stranded agreed to the only solution they could see; they extended their stay there and continued the meetings until enough money came in the offerings to get them on their way.

Finally, the long, difficult year was nearly over. They were making plans to go home to Alliance, Ohio as soon as the last concert was finished at Asbury College in Wilmore, Kentucky.

Coming out of the building after the meeting, Gladys could hardly believe what she saw.

"Look, Wilmos! My mother and father are here!" How amazing that they had driven that distance to surprise them.

Just then a little boy ran up to Wilmos, and said all in one breath, "We've been looking for our Mommy and Daddy—Daddy, I want a drink."

This little boy who could walk and talk was the baby they had not seen for a year.

Wilmos sat down on the ground and hugged him again and again, nearly overcome by the unexpected reunion.

*The Lord has already
taken my hand.*
—Wilmos Csehy

Chapter 4

For the next few years, the couple went out on their own again, as the Csehy Musical Messengers. They had learned that they were most effective when they had a singer and performed as a trio.

So they invited a series of vocalists to go with them. When one had to leave, they would find another.

Some were with them for just a short time. Geraldine Southern, whose voice they admired very much, stayed with them from 1938 to 1942.

By then World War II had made changes in the way people lived. Men were off to war; women were working at every kind of job; factories were running three shifts.

Pastors did not want to invite an evangelist to come for a week of meetings if the people were not able to attend. Since the Csehys' music was offered as part of an evangelistic ministry, there were fewer places where they could serve in that way.

Toward the end of that period they played in meetings at the Christian and Missionary Alliance Headquarters church off Times Square in New York City.

Heartstrings

As they were wondering in what direction the Lord would point them next, Dr. David Fant, pastor of that church, invited the Csehys to come and be on the staff. At the same time, their singer was invited to teach voice at the C. & M. A. college in Nyack, New York.

When they accepted that offer, they were able to have their children with them. Their home for the five years they were there was an apartment in the Bronx, in a building that was operated by a Jewish Mission belonging to the Christian and Missionary Alliance.

During those New York years, along with the ministry at the church, Wilmos taught violin to private students in his studio next to Carnegie Hall and, for two days a week, at Nyack College

For the first time they were in comfortable circumstances. They had satisfying work with the church; Wilmos' musical genius was recognized in the New York music world; they were financially secure; and they had their two growing children with them.

It was during this period that Jascha Heifetz's father heard Wilmos play. He was thrilled with his ability. He startled Wilmos by taking his hand after he had played, and kissing it all over. "Can we take you with us for the summer? We will make you into one of the world's greats."

But Wilmos told Mr. Heifetz, as he had told others before, "You can't do that. The Lord has already taken my hand."

Mr. Heifetz could not understand. How could anyone refuse such an opportunity?

"I am not giving up what the Lord called me to do," Wilmos said, knowing he would never turn his back on his calling.

And when the war was over, they knew it was time to get back on the road in full-time evangelism.

They started out again in 1947, once more leaving the children behind. This time, Richard, now eleven, went to Stony Brook School on Long Island; Wilma Jean, thirteen, went to the Montrose Girls' School in Pennsylvania.

From that time on, the family came together, for the most part, only during the summers, when

Flemington, New Jersey home of the Csehy family. this picture was taken in 1953, after they had put on an addition doubling the size of the house. Michael Csehy lived here until his death in 1972. It was headquarters for the Csehy Musical Messengers. Later daughter Jean Gelegonya and her husband stayed here, tending to things while Wilmos and Gladys were on tour.

Heartstrings

they would travel together to the Bible Conferences, and at Christmas time. It became a tradition for the Csehys to do a special Christmas program in their home church, Calvary Baptist in Flemington, New Jersey.

In his shop in Flemington, Wilmos Csehy put the finishing touches on Christmas gifts for his grandchildren, additions to a miniature village.

At the Bible conferences, while the parents were busy with their music ministry, their teenage children would be enjoying the campground activities. They especially liked going to Maranatha Bible Conference in Michigan where they formed lasting friendships.

In 1949 the couple was invited to be part of Billy Graham's first big Los Angeles tent crusade.

The big advertising banner across the entrance included the names of Beverly Shea, Cliff Barrows and Wilmos Csehy.

This crusade was the beginning of Billy Graham's unique ministry to large audiences, worldwide. It was scheduled to last for three weeks, but when the three weeks were up, he was asked to stay longer. He agreed to do so. Would the Csehys stay, also?

"We already have commitments. We wouldn't want to go back on our promises," Gladys said.

"No," Wilmos added. "The Lord has big things for Billy. I think he still wants us to go to the small places."

Billy offered to call and cancel their engagements for them, but they declined. They went on to New England, and carried out the rest of their schedule as it had been planned months before. They continued to go all around the country, wherever they were called.

Sometimes they went into meetings with well-known speakers, such as Vance Havner; other times it would be the pastor of the local church who preached. They played in Madison Square Garden for a Word of Life Rally with Jack Wyrtzen, but went just as willingly to a small country church.

It was in 1950 that they made their first recording at the RCA studios in Chicago, under Alfred B. Smith's direction. Later they did others with Smith in New York City, in Montrose, PA, and a final one in Cleveland in 1965.

Heartstrings

From time to time they added new instruments to their program. They knew of other musical groups who played glasses, and Wilmos wanted Gladys to have a set. This was not something they could send away for as they had for the bells.

The glasses that have beautiful tones are not tumblers that sit directly on the table, but glasses on raised stems. Brandy snifters provided the most melodious sounds.

They began to visit stores that sold glassware, taking a pitch pipe with them. Gladys would dip her finger in water, run it along the rim of a glass and go "Hmmm...Hmmm...Hmmm," humming to test the different notes of the scale.

"Oh, a perfect A," she would exclaim, and they would buy that glass to provide one more note of the octave.

Some notes were hard to find. As they went from one town to another, they would watch for likely places to shop for an F or a B flat. Although the natural tone of the glass could be lowered by adding the right amount of water, the tone could not be raised. So they couldn't simply buy a set and go home and tune them. Each one had to be selected individually.

It took more than a year to accumulate two octaves. Then they experimented with playing them, and very soon they were including the glasses in their concerts.

Heartstrings

Wilmos and Gladys Csehy still playing the glass harmonica in the 1960s. In the background is a new Deagan vibraharp.

With the glasses all lined up in their proper place in the octaves to form a glass harmonica, as it was called, and little containers of water handy to dip their fingers in, the two musicians produced delicate tones that caused their listeners to sit hushed, scarcely breathing.

While this was a novelty in the sense that it was an unusual instrument, the idea of playing on glasses had been around for a long time. Benjamin Franklin is credited with being the first to play them. Mozart wrote several pieces specifically for the glass harmonica.

Heartstrings

A wet finger rubbing the rim of a glass creates friction that causes the glass to vibrate, making a sound as fragile as the glass itself. The Csehys found that vinegar added to the water cut the oil on their skin, improving the contact.

Gladys, always the accompanist, played harmony on the lower notes as Wilmos played the melody. They played on this new "instrument" as professionally as they did on the more traditional ones.

On rare occasions Wilmos would play the saw. With his masterful touch, he could create beautiful tones by drawing his bow across the carpenter's tool, held between his knees, bending it more, or less, to produce higher or lower notes.

It was clear to everyone who heard them, that the Csehys enjoyed their work. It was equally clear that they were providing top quality music. They were once asked to explain how they felt about performing sacred music.

"We have not tried to glorify ourselves in showing off our skills. We should be skilled and know what we are doing, but at the same time we must get the mind of the Holy Spirit," Wilmos answered.

How did he do that?

"When I go into a service I ask the pastor what he is preaching on. Then I ask the Lord to help me build my music around the message. It is my goal to hand the program over to the evangelist or Bible teacher so that he can just take over wherever we left off. Then the Holy Spirit just dovetails it together. I believe that's the way musicianship should be."

He had no use for a pastor who expected them to entertain the congregation with their music before the serious business of the service began. He had a special dislike of having the Csehy ministry referred to as "the preliminaries." He felt so strongly about it that he would say if he were merely "preliminary" he might as well leave.

He firmly believed that the music should blend with the ministry and should be part of it—not "entertainment" and not "preliminary."

In their fifty years of service at evangelistic meetings, Bible conferences, or sacred concerts, they built their programs on conservative, traditional hymns and gospel songs, making them devotional and worshipful through brilliant, exciting arrangements.

It was also clear in their hymn arrangements and the music they selected that their preference was for classical music.

It took a brave or foolish person to ask Wilmos Csehy what he thought of "modern music." When asked about rock music, he said, "I can't stand it! Well," he added, with a twinkle in his eye, "My foot is on The Rock and my name is on the roll—I don't object to that kind of rock music."

He admitted that he liked some western music, and even disliked some classical music and some operas.

Heartstrings

Left to right: Gladys Csehy, Wilmos Csehy, Adi Cierpke, on tour in Swift Currnet, Saskatchewan. 1960s.

Several singers had traveled with them at different times. When one left them to get married in 1957, she recommended a former classmate at Tennessee Temple who had graduated as a voice major. Adi Cierpke, she told them, was in Florida working for Western Union to pay off college expenses, but her desire was to sing for the Lord.

They asked Adi to come to Flemington for an interview. As soon as they heard her beautiful lyric soprano voice and her testimony, they asked her to sing with them that weekend. She agreed.

Even with all her musical training, Adi was shy and uncomfortable. It was easy enough to talk with

Gladys, as they practiced together, but it made her nervous that Wilmos didn't say anything. He and his father just listened. She was half afraid of him.

That changed quickly, however. The three ministered together as a trio for over twenty-five years, with Wilmos becoming like a second father to Adi.

As the music of Wilmos and Gladys had blended so perfectly in the early days, audiences now heard one thought, one emotion, as this threesome sang and played together.

Before an evening meeting, Wilmos would jot down a list of pieces they might use. It wasn't terribly important, since they never referred to musical scores when they performed. (Adi did carry a "word book" just in case she had a lapse of memory.)

On the platform—perhaps before the service, or as he was playing the first number—Wilmos would "read" the faces of the audience. He would change the program to include hymns he thought would reach the people.

Sometimes he would say, "Adi, I want you to come and sing." After she got to the platform, he might still stand there a moment and think *what* he wanted her to sing. She would quickly locate the song in her word book, and by then Gladys would already be improvising an introduction.

He might play a violin obbligato as she sang. And although they had done the same song many times before, this time the obbligato might be entirely different, as Gladys' accompaniment might be new.

Heartstrings

Perhaps that is why they never tired of doing a song many times over.

At some time during each series of meetings, Wilmos would ask Adi to tell her story—how God had protected her through the bombings of Berlin and from the Russian soldiers who controlled the city. Other times he would tell of his thankfulness for God's protection and guidance in his own life.

The trio always used songs with familiar words for their instrumental numbers, and were careful not to let the melody get lost in the arrangement. They believed that words were very important, and wanted to present a message.

"Music in the church should appeal to the heart, drawing a person to a closer relationship to the Lord, rather than appealing simply to the physical emotions," Wilmos believed.

Adi, because she was presenting the words also, would sing less familiar songs. She never sang those they played as instrumental numbers. It wasn't necessary. The audience would already know those words.

Part of Gladys' brilliance as an accompanist was her ability to match the expressions of the lead musician. Audiences would marvel that she could sit down and make a beautiful arrangement of a song she had heard just once, without ever seeing the music.

Wilmos listened closely to Adi as she sang. A singer's voice is not always the same. He would stand with his head close to hers, listening to match his violin tones to the vibrato of her voice. One time, when he was doing this, a string snapped, striking her in the cheek.

Adi was stunned. Her face stung so badly that she couldn't go on. It was one of the few times in all their tours that one of them broke stride. Although distressed for the pain his instrument had inflicted, Wilmos simply picked up the extra violin he always had with him and went on playing.

By now, living on the road seemed natural to the Csehys. The trailer Wilmos had built was adapted to their special needs. He had bought a frame (axle and springs) and built on it what amounted to a giant traveling closet.

In it there were, most importantly, all the instruments they carried with them, in the special cases Wilmos had made for them. The vibraharp had to be knocked down to be packed in its case; the chimes came apart to fit into their trunklike container.

There were clothes for three of them, for all kinds of weather—because their trips would take them from the top of the country to the bottom, from one season to another in the space of a few days. He put a special partition across the front end of the trailer with a pull-out rod, so they could hang their clothes and arrive for a concert wrinkle-free.

Gladys still made all the bookings and travel arrangements. Although they shared the driving, she was chief navigator.

Heartstrings

Gladys Csehy on their first vibraharp, Wilmos Csehy with his violin, Adi Cierpke playing the Leedy chimes they purchased in the 1940s in Omaha, Nebraska.

Both of the women had had experience in making a little money stretch a long way. For these two, attractive presentable clothes to wear on the platform were a necessity.

When Gladys first went with Dr. Tucker and the Musical Messengers, her mother and some church friends took her wardrobe in hand and made or bought her four new dresses. For a long time those were all she had in which to appear night after night, each week throughout the year.

Adi had been in Berlin during the war, a young girl separated from her mother and father. When she and her sisters were finally able to come to the United States to join her parents, they were a family of eight. She, too, had learned to make the most of what was available.

Now the trailer carried a portable sewing machine and, when it was possible, they would whip up new outfits.

Sometimes they would arrive in a town just a short time before the meeting was to begin. That is when the careful organization of the trailer paid off. Instruments had to be carried in and set up. Clothing needed to be changed quickly.

Everything was in its own place, and each one knew exactly which chores were his responsibility.

Adi Cierpke, Wilmos and Gladys Csehy with the cowbells. The women are wearing dresses made by Adi. 1965.

Heartstrings

To transport their clothing, instruments and equipment, Wilmos custombuilt trailers on purchased chassis. This is an early model. McAllen, Texas 1948

The trailer used between 1962-1965. The front section held their dress clothes on a slide-out rack.

Heartstrings

They got so they could do all this in half an hour—although it took a bit longer to tune the glasses, when they were to be used.

During this time, something happened that they could never have foreseen. It was an experience that made Wilmos see his own life in a new way.

With all the miles they traveled, towing the trailer behind them, breakdowns were not unusual. This time they were in Illinois when they heard a snapping noise. The wardrobe in the front of the trailer had broken loose, and they couldn't go on until it was repaired.

Wilmos had built the trailer; he could certainly fix it. But no, the only way to get the bent metal frame straightened out was to get it red hot.

They located a welder in the town. Wilmos was a bit impatient in his early days, and no doubt he thought he could hurry things along by standing over the man as he worked.

When the rod was glowing red from the heat, it somehow slipped from the grasp of the welder's tongs. Instinctively Wilmos reached out to grab it—with his violin hand!

The burns were severe. He sat in the hospital emergency room listening as doctors wondered aloud whether he would ever again be able to play the violin with the same ability. He heard them mutter under their breath about possible nerve damage.

It was the low spot of his life. From the time he was two-and-a-half years old, a violin had been as much a part of him as his nose or his feet. It was almost like a champion runner listening to doctors planning to cut off one of his legs.

If he could not play his violin, what would he do? If he was not Wilmos Csehy the violinist, who would he be?

He had some sober conversations with God while he walked around this town far from home, looking down at his painful, bandaged hand.

When it was time to go back to the doctor, he sat in the treatment room, waiting for the doctor to examine his hand and apply new dressings. It was a dark moment. He prayed, "If you don't heal my hand, Lord, you might as well take my life. If I can't play, I can't be of any use to you."

Then in that quiet room he heard his own words and was shocked at what he had been saying. He was bargaining with—almost threatening—God. See what You are going to lose, if You don't heal me!

Was he of any value to God if he couldn't play?

Were other people who couldn't play of value to Him? Of course they were. His musical talent had come as a gift from God, but he saw that he must not demand to be in control of it.

This was the moment when Wilmos put his whole life, not just his musical life, in God's hands. As the burns healed, he determined to let God use him in whatever way he chose.

Their hostess on this particular occasion was a nurse. She worked with him to exercise his fingers.

As soon as the blisters were gone, even though the new skin was tender, he forced himself to play.

All their problems were not necessarily of a spiritual nature. In their early days on the road Gladys sometimes found herself seated at a piano that was badly out of tune. Wilmos refused to tune his violin a whole half-tone flat, so she would save the situation by playing her accompaniment in a higher key.

They were never completely happy with that solution, so they decided they must discuss this ahead of time with the churches where they would be playing. "Please have your piano tuned to the standard A-440," Gladys would tell them. From then on they had fewer unpleasant surprises of this kind.

While they enjoyed seeing the country as they traveled, there were many things they did not see. "We didn't do anything that cost money," Gladys would tell the family when they got together for the holidays.

At lunchtime they would stop at inexpensive restaurants. The violin, sensitive to changes of temperature was never left in a parked car for any length of time.

The waitress would approach them cautiously and take their order. "Anything else, sir?" she would ask, nervously eyeing the violin case that sat between Wilmos' knees. They joked that from her point of view it might contain a machine gun, or something live for which they intended to order lunch.

As with all great artists, there was more in him than he could teach.
—Samuel Hsu

Chapter 5

As the Csehys toured the country, playing in churches, schools, or summer Bible conferences, audiences found both Gladys and Wilmos warm and friendly. Teenagers were always attracted to them—especially to Wilmos.

They were fascinated by the unusual instruments—by then they used the bells, the vibraharp, the chimes, and the glasses along with the piano and violin. But the man himself drew young people like a magnet.

Wilmos playing the violin and Gladys playing the Musser vibraharp, 1960s

Heartstrings

Parents of these teenagers would ask, "Is there any place where my son can advance in his music, and be in a Christian setting?" or "How can I keep my daughter interested in playing her violin during the summer when she doesn't have lessons?"

As early as 1942 Wilmos saw the need for a summer school of music. Interlochen, in Michigan, perhaps the best-known summer music program, was a great distance for students from the east to travel.

"Isn't it sad," Wilmos would say, "that in the summer when kids have the most time to practice, their teachers hang up the fiddle and the bow and go off on vacation. The kids don't practice much until the fall, and then school comes and they don't have as much time."

He challenged his friends, "We've got to get a summer music camp going." His deep desire to start a camp or a school was a matter of prayer for twenty years as they traveled around hearing the same sort of remark.

Finally, things began to fall into place, and it looked as though they would be able to start a music school in New York State. Although that fizzled out, it made them more eager than ever to have it take place—somewhere.

For several years the Csehy Musical Messengers had been on the program at Cedar Lake Bible Conference in Indiana, about fifty miles south of Chicago. They discussed with the director,

Heartstrings

Richard Boldt, their deep interest in starting a summer school and he invited them to have it there.

How exciting it was to have this long-awaited dream coming true. Advertising for students, lining up instructors, planning the daily schedule—there was so much to do.

In their travels they had met teenage musicians who wanted to be their students. They had also met accomplished musicians who were enthusiastic about the idea of a school, and were eager to contribute their teaching skills.

Alfred Hoffsommer, from Ridley Park, Pennsylvania, was one who was eager to help get the school started. He came as an instructor the first year, and remained with the school in one capacity or another for more than thirty years. Clarke Brandt, from Greenville, Illinois, offered to be voice and choral director. Eugene Teeter, who was a percussionist and also played trombone, lived near Cedar Lake, and he agreed to come.

During their travels they had met Julius Whittinger, who had been in the United States Navy Band. He had since moved to Minnesota, but they located him there and he, also, was enthusiastic about joining them to launch the school.

With Miss Dorothy Spalding from Asbury College, Clark Brandt as voice teacher and choral director, a piano teacher from Moody Bible Institute, and of course Wilmos Csehy as director and violin instructor, the first year faculty was complete. Although Gladys Csehy did not have the title of "assistant director," it would have been appropriate, as she applied her administrative skills to pull all the details together.

They placed an ad for students in Moody Monthly magazine, hoping that those parents all across the country who had encouraged them to start the school would see it and register their children.

"How many students shall we ask the Lord for this first year?" Wilmos asked Gladys. Then, thinking they should be modest in their request, he suggested, "Let's ask Him for just a hundred."

The week before the first music camp's scheduled opening, they were at a Methodist campground in southern Illinois. They would go from there to Cedar Lake. Just before they were to leave they realized that the Lord had not sent them a hundred students. Only a handful of registrations had come in!

What should they do?

"It shouldn't be our decision," they said to each other.

It was a hot sultry day. They drove in to the nearest town and found a corner with an outdoor phone booth. Wilmos called each of the teachers.

"We have only a few students," he told them. "Shall we call it off?"

One by one, they answered, "No, don't stop now."

Heartstrings

So the Csehy Summer School of music, after twenty years of prayer, had a modest beginning at Cedar Lake Conference Grounds in 1962.

By scratching and scraping they came up with eight students—seven girls and one boy. One of the girls was Adi's sister; three others were daughters of three of the teachers.

Adi studied voice with Clark Brandt that year, and with his encouragement, taught herself teaching techniques. In later years she was the voice teacher.

That first year, school was only two weeks long. Later it was lengthened to three, then four weeks. In the following years, registrations grew steadily, if slowly, as one student told another.

Many times, the students who came would say, "We heard you play at our church back home." The thousands of miles the Csehys had traveled had made their name known across the country and was the best publicity the school could have.

Requests for information about the school came from the Midwest, from California, from New England—places they had touched in their travels.

One thing that may have helped the camp gain momentum was that high schools—in the north, more so than in the south—had bands, but rarely had orchestras. This left string musicians without any opportunity to play in a group. A camp where they could play in an orchestra appealed to them.

Heartstrings

Wilmos and Gladys had a vision for a unique music school, and the actual school, as it came into being, matched the vision.

In Wilmos' own words, the object of the school was "...to give a place where young people, first of all, can come under the influence of listening to good things—not only spiritual things (that's what this camp is definitely based on) but on good fundamental basic music.

"We don't allow them to bring their recorded tapes, we don't allow them to bring radios. We have no TV. We are trying to focus their minds on the better things.

"The musical environment as far as we can determine and control is of the highest quality."

They saw it as a 50/50 mix of music and Christianity. And that is roughly the way the program began and has continued. However, the Christian influence may actually be greater, as the example of the instructors' lives could not possibly be separated from their music.

Because advertising was done primarily in Christian magazines and by word of mouth, most students came from Christian backgrounds. But not all. While the Csehys believed that each person needed to know Jesus Christ as Savior in a personal, life-changing way, there was no pressure on a student to make that decision. Campers who came from other religious backgrounds were made to feel comfortable.

All of them, however, were required to attend

morning chapel, evening Sing Time, and devotions led by the dorm counselors.

In the thirty-minute chapel session, a different Bible teacher spoke each week. This provided good, solid Bible teaching—familiar to some, new to others.

Counselors were to make themselves available to the students at any time of the day. For it was often in private talks, the Csehys believed, that a seed sown in chapel would begin to sprout.

Dorm devotions were warm, intimate sessions, where the young musicians shared their frustrations, discoveries and hopes, and learned to pray their way through them.

Janet Rawleigh, after she had been on the faculty as woodwinds instructor for several years, said, "When I was a camper, the devotions we had with our counselor were my favorite part of camp. We would talk about how we felt when we were performing or things we'd experienced in our lessons."

And then she added, "But Sing Time was a close second."

Sing Time brought the whole group—faculty, staff and students—together for an impromptu program. It always included singing, of course. There might be instrumental music. There might be a testimony bubbling out of a camper who had put new trust in the Lord. There might be a surprise performance by a student. There would be Uncle Wilmos sharing his thoughts about how the Lord wanted to be close to each one of them.

Heartstrings

It was a moving experience for the young students and accomplished instructors to come together in this relaxed, nightly gathering. Here they could enjoy the music and each other without any sense of competition.

Sing Time ended the same way each evening. Referring to the campers as he always thought of them, Uncle Wilmos would say, "Good night, Sweethearts!"

They heard his love for them in this oft-repeated phrase and remembered it as a sort of benediction.

In some respects, Csehy Summer School of Music was similar to other good Christian camps.

It was the music half of the Csehy formula that made it unique. Wilmos Csehy had very high standards of musicianship—for himself and his students.

His own first teacher, his father, had been thorough and painstaking. He had taught him the importance of using correct techniques; he had taught him to develop the self-discipline a musician must have; and he had taught him to enjoy music.

This is what Wilmos wanted to pass on to his students.

"Aspiring Christian musicians should strive for excellence," he insisted. "They should get the best training possible. You don't get it on an hour a day of practice."

He thought that to be mediocre was not good enough. "High quality and excellence are honoring to the Lord."

While he, himself, felt called to a full-time ministry in music, he repeated often that Christians have every right to be "professional musicians", performing in symphony orchestras or as soloists, appearing on radio or television, teaching in schools or giving private lessons, as long as doing so did not in any way conflict with their Christian testimony.

He also wanted to pass on an appreciation of "good" music. To Wilmos that meant conservative, traditional hymns and gospel songs and secular classical music.

"A Christian musician should be a leader and set standards of producing good music of high quality," he stated.

There were skeptics who didn't think teenagers who were constantly bombarded by contemporary music would accept Wilmos' definition of good music.

One minister said to him, "You know I don't like this contemporary music. But I guess it's what the young people want, so we just have to go along with it."

"No," Wilmos told him, "it's not what they want; it's all they know. It is up to us to show them something better."

Was he right about that? Did they come to appreciate what he felt was "good" music? The enthusiasm they put into singing the songs he chose for Sing Time answers the question.

Dr. Sam Hsu, piano instructor and board member at the school explains their acceptance of the classics by saying, "It was just the power of the music."

Wes White says, "Even terribly corny songs from the 1940s—when Wilmos led the singing, they loved it. They knew he was out of touch with the times musically, but no one bucked it because of their love for him."

One student, when exposed to Wilmos' taste in classical music, commented, "If a piece of music has lasted 300 years, it's important enough to listen to."

Although Wilmos demanded excellence of himself and his students, it was not his goal to steer all of them into careers in music.

Some, of course, came without the talent to make it their profession. Others lacked a sufficiently strong drive to see them through the hours of practice needed to master their instruments.

Still others, with remarkable talent and a real desire to go as far as they could with their music, felt God calling them in other directions.

How did Wilmos feel when a very talented young musician chose to go into medicine, or teaching, or pastoral work, or to the mission field?

According to Dr. Hsu he would say, "'Be the best musician you can be, by the grace of God.'

"Wilmos was realistic about our world. He would be sad only if you wandered from following Jesus. If you followed Him, he knew that the Lord was leading your life. He rejoiced in that."

The lodge at Cedar Lake
The Csehy School's first home

*He was respected in the musical community
for his mastery of classical music.*
—Wesley White

Chapter 6

The Csehy Summer Music Camp was established and growing—outgrowing its space at Cedar Lake. "We really need more rooms for teaching," the Csehys said, as they discussed the problem.

Private lessons were offered on a variety of instruments, and the instructors needed a place to give those lessons. The students needed practice rooms. There was equipment to be stored from summer to summer.

The camp needed a home that could adapt to its needs. At Cedar Lake they were one of many groups sharing the grounds.

By 1968 the camp was running for four weeks in the summer. The rest of the year the Csehys continued their music ministry all across the country.

For the past two years, 1966 and 1967, they had traveled to a Bible conference near Muncy,

Heartstrings

Pennsylvania called Ashurst Manor. The owner there wanted to build up the conference, and brought in some well-known speakers and musicians to attract people.

When Wilmos mentioned to him that he was looking for new quarters for his school, he was invited to bring it to Ashurst.

Wilmos would not do that without careful consideration on both sides. "You come out to Cedar Lake and see our school in operation," he suggested. "Then we can decide."

He had some doubts of his own. Ashurst was an attractive, wooded property where he enjoyed listening to the birds. Often he would surprise a deer when he was out for his morning walks. The majestic trees added to his appreciation of God's creation.

But was it the right place for the school?

They had begun by calling it a camp, for it was held in a typical camp setting. By now they were thinking of it and advertising it as the Csehy Summer School of Music. In the middle of Pennsylvania's hills, would it draw as many students as it would if it were closer to the big eastern cities? Would the people living in rural Pennsylvania appreciate classical music and support the school?

The village of Muncy, a mile down the road, had charm, history dating back to the Revolutionary War, and a population of less than 3,000.

Thirteen miles to the west, Williamsport, ten times the size of Muncy, was the area's hub of business, industry, and culture. But people from the New York and Philadelphia metropolitan areas, if they had heard of these places at all, considered them to be "somewhere up in the boondocks." Would they travel that far to a music school?

"I'm just not sure that's where God wants us," Wilmos said, trying, as always, to be sure of God's direction before moving ahead.

Ashurst's director did go to Indiana to observe the school in session, as Wilmos had suggested. He must have been amazed at what he saw—a choir, a band, an orchestra, instrumental soloists—all high school students!

"Bring this to Pennsylvania! Bring it to Ashurst!" he begged them.

By then the Csehys were confident that this was the new home God had selected for the school, and they agreed.

Tom and Ruth Burns, two staunch backers of the Csehy School, helped to move them to the new location. They were ready to welcome students there in the summer of 1968.

The beautiful Victorian manor house, sitting on a hill above the Susquehanna River, was the centerpiece of the conference grounds. Built in 1861, it had been sold by the Ashurst heirs to Pennsylvania Senator Charles W. Sones, who lived there for a time. Before it was sold to become a conference ground, the last owner had turned it into a commercial inn.

Down a slope, off to one side, was a small house, probably at one time used for servants. An old icehouse had been converted to living quarters, and the former carriage house was now an assembly hall. A new building, just completed, was large enough to have a dormitory upstairs and a meeting room downstairs.

What they found at their new home was not instant perfection. Nor were there enough buildings for all their needs. But there were 31 acres on which to expand—sometime.

Four of the staff and their wives crowded into the little servants' house. Alfred Hoffsommer lived on the first floor; the Csehys took a room on the second floor; the Petersons, whom they had gotten to know in Cedar Lake, lived in the other first floor room. Dolores Peterson (who became known as Lady P) was the head dorm mother.

The little house, called Bethany, was not only their home during the school term, but their studio as well. Mr. Hoffsommer gave cello lessons downstairs, Wilmos taught violin in their bedroom, and from another second-floor bedroom came the sounds of Eugene Teeter's trombone.

Band, orchestra and choir rehearsals were held on the lower level of the boys' dorm.

It was tight quarters, but a beginning. They fit themselves into these buildings and dreamed of additions they would like to make.

No one was quite sure how the move from Cedar Lake would affect the growth of the school. They constantly had to turn to God for their financial needs.

But these experiences knit the Csehys and their teaching staff even more closely together. They were dedicated to a common goal. Many of the people who were part of the early struggle to keep the school going stayed with it for ten years, some twenty or more.

Wilmos envisioned an outdoor amphitheater on the terraced slope that fell away from the back of the Manor House toward the river. He found that the owner had already started building a band shell at the foot of it, and he was disappointed that work was too far along for him to tell them how it should be built. But he was encouraged to see that improvements were being made.

The second year, for teaching rooms they rented three little trailers—"empty boxes with doors in them," Gladys called them. They would make do with these until they could afford to build.

For three years, the Csehys conducted camp at Ashurst Manor, then went back on the road for the other eleven months, as they had done when the camp was at Cedar Lake. It was a relief to have a permanent home for the school, a place to leave things from one year to the next.

The trailer upgraded once again. Wilmos and Gladys Csehy, Adi Cierpke, 1973

One fall day, in 1970, Tom Burns made a trip up to Ashurst Manor from his home in New Jersey to help out with maintenance work, as he often did.

He was dumbfounded to find that the property was listed for sheriff's sale. The owner had not been able to pay back all the money he had borrowed to make improvements.

The sale was only a few days off, and the Csehys were somewhere out on the road—Tom wasn't sure where. He would have to act for them. The Sheriff's Office seemed the place to start.

"We've got a problem, here," Tom told the sheriff. He explained that there were things on the property that belonged to the Csehy School.

To his relief, the sheriff gave him permission to remove anything that belonged to the Csehys, but that was easier said than done. He had to rent an 18-wheeler to load all of their things—chairs, music stands, music, all kinds of things—and haul them back to his home in New Jersey. He kept the loaded trailer there until the spring.

It seemed as though the school had lost its home. But at the sheriff's sale, no one came up with a bid high enough to buy the property.

It was not only the Csehys and their faculty who were concerned about what would happen to Ashurst. Many people had given or loaned money to keep the place afloat as a Christian conference ground. A group of business people who cared about the place, including some who had already loaned money they would never get back, met to see what could be done.

There were about twenty in the group that agreed to buy the property back from the mortgage holder at a cost of $130,000. Some of these were supporters of the music school. Not wealthy people, they agreed to put up their homes to guarantee the loan.

Heartstrings

Clyde Weigle headed this group of investors, and a non-profit corporation, Muncy Terraces Christian Activity Center, came into being.

By the time Wilmos and Gladys came back to hold camp in 1971, both the ownership and the name of the place had changed.

The school found creative ways to stretch the space. Mrs. Csehy would show pictures of these early days at Muncy Terraces and say, "See that building over there? That's the trailer Tom Burns rented to rescue our things.

"He rented it, then bought it for two dollars. He cut windows and doors in it, put a roof over it, and divided it into three rooms. One room is a flute studio, one a clarinet studio and the other is used for storage."

When asked why most of the buildings had names on them, but that one did not, Mrs. Csehy would explain, "Oh, we used to call it Uncle Tom's Cabin, but someone decided that might be considered a slurring remark, so we took the sign down."

The new board of Muncy Terraces Christian Activity Center hired a director for the conference grounds, and the Csehys continued their pattern of school in the summer, travel in winter.

In the early years, practice pianos were loaned by the Baldwin Piano Company through Taylor Music Store in Willow Grove, Pennsylvania. Eventually through gifts or bargain buys they purchased their own instruments, accumulating more than twenty.

In 1978 they renovated the old icehouse, which became Adi Cierpke's home. Fittingly, she named it Jenny Lind.

Gradually more buildings were added. Weigle Chapel could hold 500 for concerts, or could be used as a gym. Several motel units were acquired to house the school staff. In 1983, Spalding Lane was created, with tiny practice cabins lining each side. This was possible because of a bequest from former faculty member, Dorothy Spalding.

The balance of her gift was put towards the purchase of the Baldwin Concert Grand piano that was being retired by the Academy of Music in Philadelphia. Adi Cierpke succeeded in raising another $8,000 to meet the price of $12,000. This significant addition to the equipment of the school was given in honor of the Csehys' 50th wedding anniversary.

Young people were coming to them now from all around the country, finding something that filled an empty place in their lives.

Diana Schmuck, who later became one of the school's piano instructors, first came to Csehy with her twin sister when she was a tenth grader. She was excited about music, but not quite sure that she could really be a musician.

Heartstrings

"My first impression on arriving at Muncy Terraces was that this was one big family, and I didn't belong!" Very quickly, however, she did feel a part of it.

"I had never realized how much loving one another was part of Christianity. Living together in the dorm we had to learn to deal with all kinds of problems. Uncle Wilmos established that attitude." Diana marks her student days at Csehy as an important part of her spiritual growth.

Janet Rawleigh is another of the school's instructors who had been a camper at Csehy. She had been to other Christian camps and thought she knew what it would be like. Three things surprised her.

For one, the mountains took her breath away. They were such a contrast to the flatness of Iowa, where she lived.

Then she was amazed at Wilmos' mastery of the violin. She had never before heard double stops—two notes played at one time. Quickly she discovered there was tremendous talent among the other campers, as well.

Most of all, she was surprised at how friendly the campers were, and she was impressed by the strong personal faith they showed. She saw others her own age who placed great importance on what Christ had done in their lives. The most popular ones showed the strongest commitment to Christian living. "...even the boys!" she would say, astonished. She had accepted Christ at a young age, but had a significant growth spurt at Csehy.

"If I had anything like homesickness, it was really a desire to be part of it all."

*The violin was obedient to him
because of his skills.*
—Samuel Hsu

Chapter 7

Csehy campers were all students who had a strong interest in pushing ahead with their music studies. In order to be accepted in the school they had to have a letter from their music teacher recommending them and, for those who played band or string instruments, a recommendation from their band or orchestra leader.

Even so, they came with far different levels of achievement. Some were top-ranking solo performers, while others were barely able to keep up, but that didn't bother the instructors. Trying to improve was what counted.

Their attitude filtered down to the students themselves. Someone who had a lot to learn about trumpet playing did not feel disgraced if his bunkmate could play rings around him.

Janet Rawleigh confirms that wherever you were musically, you fit in. "It didn't matter what level you had reached."

Heartstrings

Wilmos Csehy's joy was in teaching young students.

Diana Schmuck remembers a concert performance when she was still unsure of her own ability. Wilmos put his arm around her, turned to the audience and said, "Just wait and hear what she does in ten years!"

Lillian Pinkham, who has been on the staff of Csehy as counselor, or dorm mother, or secretary for many years, explains it this way: "He appreciated the best, and yet he took the least, and had time for them."

Lillian has a favorite story about her son Timmy when he was a four-year-old and was with her at the school. Although much too young to be a registered student, he was beginning to learn to play a violin and wanted very badly to be in one of the concerts. He was a long way from concert level, but he begged to play.

Wilmos knew of his great desire and arranged a duet so that they could play together, giving him his moment on stage. Timmy plinked the few notes of Silent Night assigned to him, accompanied by the rich sounds of the master violinist.

"That was Wilmos' heart," said Timmy's mother.

There were only one or two times when a young person who applied to the school had to be turned down. This was not because anyone and everyone would be accepted, but because the application form itself weeded out those who were not qualified.

It asked such questions as, how many years have you been taking lessons on your instrument? What piece have you most recently mastered?

Where have you performed publicly? Only advanced students were able to give satisfactory answers.

If they were poor students or beginners they—or at least their parents—would realize that they were not Csehy material. And they would not be able to send in that necessary letter from their band leader if they were not at a level to benefit from the intense musical training of the Csehy School.

When applications began to come in each year, it was an exciting time for Wilmos and Gladys. They were always delighted when there was a note included saying they knew someone who had been to the school and were applying because of the good things they had been told about it.

When an application came from someone who hadn't heard about it from another student, usually they—or their parents—had seen an ad in a Christian magazine.

"Listen to this!" Gladys said to Wilmos one day. It was a most unusual application, from a twelve-year-old girl.

"She is far too young," he said.

At this time, they had not yet started a junior high session. Only senior high school students were accepted.

"But there are special circumstances," she told him, showing him the letter from Mr. and Mrs. Fung.

His eye caught the name of Ivan Galamian, one of the most prominent violin teachers in the world, and he sat down to read the letter from its beginning.

Their daughter's violin teacher wanted her to go to Meadowmount School in New York state to study with Mr. Galamian, but it would be for an eight-week session.

They had seen an ad for the Csehy School in the Moody Monthly magazine, the letter said. Since their daughter was so young, they would feel much better about sending her to a Christian music camp that was only four weeks long, and not quite so far from her home in Ohio.

"Even though she is under your age limit, would you please consider taking Molly as a student?" the Fungs asked.

"I don't know that we ought to do that," Gladys said. "But take a look at her application."

They learned that Molly had been enrolled in the Suzuki program at Oberlin College at the age of 3-1/2.

"I don't have any use for the Suzuki method," Wilmos commented.

He read on. She was performing solo by the time she was eight. Since the age of six, when the family had moved to Cleveland, she had been taught in the traditional method.

"Well, then maybe she has learned the important basics," he muttered.

"They sent two tapes," Gladys said, turning to their tape player. One was Molly playing alone; on the other she was playing duets with a friend. When they heard the music, they knew they were listening to a skilled violinist.

Heartstrings

"Oh, let's have her come," Wilmos said.

But it would present some problems. There is a lot of difference between a twelve-year-old and a fourteen-year-old. Would she fit in? Would the other students accept her? She was a child, really, and they were not set up to handle children.

"Well, both of the girls applied," Gladys pointed out. "Maybe if they came together, it wouldn't be so hard for them." They had doubts, though. The other girl was only ten.

"We'll take them both," Wilmos decided.

On her birthday the Csehys welcome Molly Fung and her mother, Lorna Fung. (Photograph by Philip H. C. Fung.)

When the two girls arrived, it took everyone by surprise how little they were. Molly was tiny and her oriental features made her seem like a live doll to the husky teenage boys.

Molly was frightened at being away from home for the first time. She didn't expect the other campers to accept anyone so much younger. But before she knew it, the big boys were carrying the two of them around on their shoulders like toys or mascots. She felt like a favorite little sister. They didn't care how old—or young—she was.

Then came the moment when Wilmos had her play her violin for them.

Janet Rawleigh remembers, "When I heard her it just blew me away."

To their acceptance and love, her fellow students now added respect. But Molly Fung's first year at Csehy was still going to be a challenging experience. It was designed to be that for all students.

"How can Uncle Wilmos do those amazing things on his violin—without any music?" she wondered.

She knew she could not read music as well as many of the others, because much of her training had been in the Suzuki method. She had never played in an orchestra, yet here she was expected to do that. This was frightening to her and she mentioned it during Sing Time.

Uncle Wilmos put his arm around her, right then and there, and said, "We'll work on this in your lesson."

She discovered that his violin lessons covered a lot more than how to produce perfect tones. They included making music fun and challenging.

One day Molly listened to a boy who was badly off pitch. Wilmos didn't tell him that. He said, "That's not just quite right. Let's go back and take a look at it. Let's do it together."

The man was like a loving grandfather to the girl who had not been at all sure she belonged with these teenagers. She felt especially close to Uncle Wilmos because of the love they both had for the violin.

So, when he told her that she was to perform at the Saturday night outdoor concert, she trusted him. But it was a difficult Bach suite that he gave her to play. She couldn't help being a little afraid, even though she had practiced diligently.

"And I think we'll have you do that without any accompaniment," Uncle Wilmos told her.

She had soloed many times before, but somehow playing here, before the other campers and instructors and visiting music lovers, and before Uncle Wilmos made her determined to do her best.

The amphitheater on the terrace was a lovely place for the audience to listen to a concert. They could look out at the sunset; they could enjoy cool evening breezes; and they could appreciate the tall evergreen trees that bordered the seating area and the old apple trees near the stage.

But Molly quickly discovered that the outdoor band shell was a difficult place to play. She could barely hear her own notes in that vast open space.

Then, just as she was beginning to feel comfortable performing in these strange surroundings, something landed with a thud on the platform, and rolled across, toward the center, stopping less than a yard from Molly's feet. The attention of everyone in the audience was on the fallen apple that seemed sure to interrupt her performance. They all watched, waiting to see what she would do.

She went right on playing.

The beaming look on Uncle Wilmos' face as he hugged her at the end of her piece was proof that her performance had pleased him.

The Csehys never regretted their decision to accept Molly Fung as a student. When she was a few years older she did go to study with Ivan Galamian, but also spent time at The Csehy School.

"My heart was at Csehy," she says, "probably because of the friendships I made there that made music come alive."

Wilmos encouraged her in every area, but never pressured her toward a career in music. "The Lord has given you a gift," he told her. "I hope you will use that gift." Then he hastened to add, "I think you are doing that. I just don't want you to ever forget that the Lord gave you this. And it's the biggest gift He could give. This is His voice for you."

As he came to respect Molly's playing, his attitude toward the Suzuki method softened, but he still felt it needed to be combined with traditional instruction.

It was a joy for the Csehys to have Molly as one of their students, but others came who presented problems. They would come without respect for authority or, as Wes White did, rebelling against the Christian lifestyle.

"Some went out the way they came in, but very few of them," Wilmos said. He mentioned letters he had received from parents who appreciated the change in their teenagers after a month at Csehy.

And some—a very, very few—were asked to leave. Only those closest to him knew that Wilmos wept over those.

Mrs. Csehy and Lillian Pinkham were at their wits' end with one boy and decided to call Wilmos in to deal with his behavior. The women told him of the serious rule the boy had broken, hoping that he would send him home immediately.

Wilmos looked at the boy sadly and said, "If what they tell me is true, you have broken my heart." Then he turned and started to walk away.

"What do you want us to do?" Gladys called after him.

"Do whatever you want."

Knowing Wilmos' great love for each one of the teenagers, and how hard it was for him to give up on any of them, they found some other way to discipline this boy.

He stayed on for the rest of the term, observing Christian principles in action. That student learned that the rules were to be obeyed. And he learned that he was deeply loved.

I play the classics in church.
—Wilmos Csehy

Chapter 8

When the Csehy School was first started, the musicians who joined Wilmos Csehy to make up the faculty were people who had been inspired by his vision. They all had deep faith as well as being expert musicians. More than that, they wanted to pass on to young people their love of God and their love of good music.

None of them would have taken the job just for the small salary that was offered—salary that would be paid only if there were money at the end of the summer with which to pay it. They did it to serve the Lord.

After the excitement of starting a new school was past, the struggles to keep it afloat went on. While it continued to grow, each year they wondered how they would make ends meet. The instructors were paid, but never an amount equal to what they could have earned elsewhere.

Heartstrings

In spite of that there were always new people ready to fill the places left by those who were not able to return. Perhaps it was because of the Csehys' total trust that new instructors were always available when they were needed. Some came in what seemed the most casual ways.

For instance, Dr. Virginia Brubaker had been teaching piano at Csehy, but in 1974 she was not able to return. She recommended, as her replacement, Samuel Hsu. He had formerly been her student, but was then a fellow piano teacher at Philadelphia College of Bible. Wilmos and Gladys relied on her recommendation.

Dr. Brubaker said to Sam, "I suggested your name to the Csehys. I won't be able to go this summer and they will need someone to take my place."

Mr. Hsu had never visited the school, nor had he met the Csehys, but shortly after that he had a telephone call from them. Over the phone it was arranged that he would come and teach.

He didn't know what to expect when he was picked up at the small Lycoming airport and driven to Muncy Terraces. As they drove past the tall pines that lined the road into camp, Sing Time was in progress.

"I was impressed by the body of Christian musicians singing lustily," Sam says. "I never felt that the grounds were fantastic. But the atmosphere! Driving in over the dusty road, you immediately felt the difference. I always loved it.

"There is a deep sense of God's presence. God chooses to work in the limited environment. We are not on a Club Med vacation. As long as we are comfortable, no one complains. The facilities are a dimension in the Lord's dealing you have to accept."

Nor had the Csehys known what to expect in Sam.

When they came to know him first-hand, it was clear that the Lord had chosen to send an exceptional man to them.

Sam Hsu had wanted to play the piano since he first heard the one in their Presbyterian church in Shanghai when he was a little boy. He began his lessons when he was nine years old. His aunt prayed about his musical education and arranged for him to audition at the Shanghai Conservatory, where he then went to study.

He came to the United States in 1965 to attend Philadelphia College of Bible. After graduating he went on to the University of California for further music studies, and then returned to PCB to teach piano.

His musicianship was a feather in the cap of the Csehy School; his faith was a strong support. He continued to come back year after year, eventually becoming a board member. He would have had no difficulty filling his summer with concert tours, but he chose to use his gift of music at Csehy.

A few years later, Dale Shepfer who was orchestra and band director at the time, mentioned to a friend that the school was in need of a choral director.

The friend, David Shockey, accepted that position in 1977. He smiles, remembering the pay he earned—$30-$35 a week. "But I fell in love with Wilmos and Gladys. They were unusual people who conducted the camp because they felt a clear calling. It made the camp distinctive."

Eleanor Shockey taught piano and accompanied the choir her husband directed. Their love for the Csehys, for the faculty and for the students called them back year after year.

Many years before that, when there had been a gap in the faculty, the Csehys had received a letter from a man in Oregon asking if they could use someone with his qualifications.

Clarke Potter explained that two or three years earlier, he had seen their ad for students in Moody Monthly and liked the idea of a Christian music school. He had kept the ad all that time until he had a summer free so he could apply. Again, as they accepted him and learned to know him, they knew he had been sent by the Lord.

Another teacher came by a quite different route—through Janet Cochran who had been a camper, then a counselor, then head counselor, then oboe instructor. Csehy had become so much a part of her that she called herself a "lifer".

She found herself involved in a serious romantic relationship with another musician. When he began to talk about marriage, she wanted him to understand the things that were most important to her. "Csehy, for one thing," she told him.

"What's that?"

He heard from her all about The Csehy Summer School of Music. He also understood the message tucked between the words: If he wanted her, he would have to take the Csehy School as well.

At her suggestion he went to check the place out for himself—and was hooked. Floyd Rawleigh became instructor in voice and theory, and later a member of the board of directors. And also Janet's husband.

He shares her goal: To make sure God's work continues at Csehy. Specifically, that means to them, "Keeping spiritual conditions consistent and mixing together the greatest and the least in musical ability."

Molly Fung had created a stir when she first appeared as a twelve-year-old camper. She had been amazed at the freedom and creativity with which Wilmos played the violin. Then as she went on with her own studies, she realized that the things he did were skills she could learn.

The time came when, in planning a concert, Wilmos would say, "Let's have Molly do that. She can do a better job on that than I can."

When Molly was in high school she divided her time between the Csehy and Meadowmount Camps. Meadowmount gave strong technical training for only the most advanced violinists. By the time she had graduated from high school, it would have been understandable if she had been too busy with her musical career to think of returning to Csehy.

But she was delighted to return as violin instructor during her college years, considering it an honor to teach from Ye Olde Fiddle Shoppe, the studio where Uncle Wilmos had instructed her.

"I have kept the friends I made at the other camp, but my heart was at Csehy," she says.

She mentions two things that tie her to the Csehy School—the strong friendships based on mutual Christian faith, and learning from her piano lessons with Sam Hsu to enjoy music.

She was nearly as uneasy about returning as an instructor as she was about arriving that first year as an underage camper. She was still a college student. Would the faculty accept her as one of them?

They not only accepted her, but tried in every way to help her get used to her new role.

While the people who make up the faculty have changed through the years, they have all been committed to the same goals. This makes for close bonds between them.

Several faculty members found romance at Csehy. And there are former campers, now married, where both husband and wife have fond memories of being students at the school.

Some look forward to Csehy summers as much for being with the other faculty members as for the teaching they will do.

Instructors bring their families to stay on the grounds with them, feeling as Janet Rawleigh does, that it is a wonderful experience for them. The children are well cared for. They benefit from contact with the students, the babysitters, and the other faculty parents. "They are exposed to both music and discipline that is good for the whole family," she says.

Some of the faculty were closer to Wilmos than others. To a few he was able to confide the grave financial troubles that kept cropping up. Others knew only that he trusted the Lord for every need, and they were not aware of specific problems until he asked them to rejoice with him that a need had been met.

*My Father in heaven is rich…so I have
every right to come and ask Him.*
—Wilmos Csehy

Chapter 9

In 1978 the director of Muncy Terraces became ill and the board searched without success for someone to replace him.

"If you can't find anyone, we'll come and do it," Wilmos Csehy told them.

"No, you don't understand. We must have someone who will be here all year long. You wouldn't give up your concert tours to come and do that, would you?"

Wilmos Csehy did not make hasty decisions. He was sure the Lord was directing him to this work, as He had long ago called him to a music ministry.

"Yes. We would."

He might have been hoping there would be time to indulge some of his hobbies. Because for all his dedication to music, he had many other interests.

He was fond of hunting and fishing. At Muncy Terraces he would be in the right setting to enjoy outdoor hobbies. He discovered that the opening day of deer season was a local holiday with schools and many businesses closed. Even if his duties kept

Heartstrings

Wilmos with his beagles. 1957

him from doing these things, a sportsman enjoys just being out of doors. At Muncy, it was all there at the door of his trailer.

The birds were his friends. He knew them all. They sang to him from the trees that surrounded him and taught him melodies to play back on his violin. His recording of "His Eye is on The Sparrow" delights every one who hears it.

During his days in New York he had learned to repair violins. Now that he would no longer be touring during the winter, there would be long evenings that he could spend working on the instruments that had been left with him for repairs.

Heartstrings

Repairing musical instruments was one of Wilmos' favorite hobbies.

Heartstrings

His fingers could use a paintbrush as well as a violin bow. Perhaps there would be time for painting or the lapidary work he enjoyed so much.

But perhaps not.

With so much to do—the Csehy School to run, the conference ground to develop—Wilmos' schedule in 1978 was full.

This time it was not filled with exhausting cross-country tours—although they would still be giving concerts close to home—but with pressures of a different kind.

As he took over the direction of Muncy Terraces he had some unpleasant surprises. Banks did not want to lend money; businesses in the community did not want to deal with him. They remembered unpaid bills.

Many local churches were unsympathetic. They were still smarting from disagreements with past directors. Even folks who wished them well wondered if people would ever forget that the main building had once been a rather rowdy tavern.

Wilmos Csehy was a godly man, a gifted musician, and a jack-of-most-other-trades. He was not an administrator, not a businessman, not a wheeler-dealer. Gladys had always handled their money.

Along with the disappointment of discovering that there was not enough money coming in to meet expenses, there came a feeling of shame that other Christians could be less than fair and open in the way they did business.

Although Muncy Terraces and the Csehy School were separate organizations (The school had incorporated in 1961), their fates were intertwined. What would be good for one should be good for both. What damaged one would damage both. Things over which he had no control were reflecting badly on the name of the school.

A week after taking on this new job, Wilmos landed in the Muncy Valley Hospital with a severe heart attack.

Would this have happened if everything had been going smoothly? No one knows. People who were close to him saw a direct connection.

After four weeks in the hospital, he was ordered to take another three months of recovery time at home. Finally he was allowed to take up his duties—but with his doctor's lists of dos and don'ts to hamper him.

He tried to follow these rules—at least the ones he thought were reasonable. He kept to a schedule that got him to bed on time, and he watched his diet carefully.

One rule, however, was simply not acceptable. "No more violin playing. It's going to kill you."

This edict was understandable to anyone who stood near him when he played, as Adi Cierpke often did. "He played so hard," she says. "He would play with his feet apart for balance. He came down with his heels. He poked holes in his socks with his toes." He played with his heart, his mind, and his body.

Heartstrings

Wilmos played with his heart, his mind, and his body (Photograph by Philip H. C. Fung).

He tossed that foolish rule out the window, for the violin was what gave significance to his life. There were other ways to save his energy.

That's when he got a motor-scooter to cover the miles back and forth across the campus that were all part of his day's work.

It was clear that they would have to operate on an even tighter budget, and he took more and more of the physical work upon himself. He would motor-scoot from a violin lesson at his studio down to the swimming pool to repair a pump, back up to the dorm to check on a counselor who was not feeling well, then across to the manor house for lunch.

The scooter was his compromise with the doctor's list of no-nos.

Diana Schmuck chuckles at the picture of this big round man, wearing a little round hat, scooting along with his dog, Candy, scampering along beside him. He would drive up beside someone and stop to talk, just as he had formerly walked with his arm around them.

Apparently convinced that he must single-handedly change people's opinion of Muncy Terraces, he found it hard to turn over any duties to someone else.

One of the faculty members felt this had not been good for either Wilmos or the school, saying, "You can only go so far on one person's personality.

"As director of the school, he was actually responsible for every part of it. That would have been a full time job, but he would also have fifteen to twenty violin students who would each have two half-hour lessons a week; he would supervise the counselors; he would conduct morning chapel; he would lead Sing Time each night; he would oversee meals, beginning them with a song and prayer. This would have been a strain on a healthy man."

For five years he kept Muncy Terraces Christian Activity Center active through the spring, fall and winter months. For a long time he also drove three hours each way, twice a week, to teach violin at Philadelphia College of Bible.

And during the six weeks when the Csehy Summer School of Music was in session he worked like a one-man army.

All year long they also were broadcasting "Golden Gems of Sacred Melody." The half hour program aired each Saturday morning over Christian radio station, WPGM, in Danville.

"It was too much for him. He couldn't have gone on without somehow adjusting his own position," says Wes White. "The financial responsibility of the school weighed heavily on him. He needed to be freed from that to be the visionary."

He was freed from it on October 5, 1983, when he went to be with the Lord he had served.

Just three months before, with his heart becoming weaker and weaker, Wilmos and Gladys Csehy celebrated their 50th year of marriage. And in that same year they received the Distinguished Christian Leadership Award of the Philadelphia College of Bible.

He was aware that his time was running out and tried to prepare his "family".

They had just purchased a new trailer. Since 1978 they had been living in an eight-foot-wide-trailer that their son Richard had helped them purchase. Now they felt the need for more elbow room, and they selected one that was twelve feet wide. Wilmos slept in it only one night, when he had a second heart attack.

The front entrance to the trailer had not yet been put in place, so he had to be carried through the back door to the ambulance that would take him to the hospital.

He did not return to his new home. The heart attack he suffered in the hospital the following day was fatal.

ᴔᴔ ᴔᴔ ᴔᴔ ᴔᴔ

Camp opened in 1984 with Gladys Csehy as director.

The faculty and returning campers appreciated and respected her leadership. But there was a missing element—Wilmos' personality.

It was most noticeable at Sing Time at the end of the day, where Uncle Wilmos had always opened his heart to them. That was when they had shared spontaneous prayers and testimonies, when they had seen him weep when students told how camp had changed their lives. It was there that they waited, after the benediction, wanting to hear the familiar, "Good night, Sweethearts."

For Gladys it was more than the loss of a husband; it was the loss of the one who had been her partner in music for fifty years.

Heartstrings

For Adi Cierpke, it was the loss of someone who had been almost like a father. For Molly Fung, it was the loss of a dear friend.

"It was as though camp had been a child and Wilmos the father," Diana Schmuck said. "When he died the camp was an adolescent—struggling, but not yet mature. We wondered at first if it could continue without him. Or rather, how the responsibilities would be shared out."

"Will the philosophy of Wilmos Csehy continue?" they asked each other. "By the grace of God it will," Sam Hsu declared.

Ashurst Manor
The Csehy School's second home
was renamed Muncy Terraces.

*His musical genius translates
(his emotion) into violin song.*
—Music Critic
Toronto Telegram

Chapter 10

There were many memories of Wilmos that surfaced when he was no longer there. His friends told each other things they already knew, just to relive the events that included him.

"Remember the day we came in late to chapel?" someone asked sheepishly.

Easy-going as he was as an administrator, there were some things that annoyed him—like people coming in late to a concert. He might not be able to control that, but he saw no excuse for a counselor to be late for chapel. The tardy ones recalled that they had slipped in as inconspicuously as possible a few minutes after the service began. Wilmos said nothing then, but he had all the counselors—those who had been on time as well as those who were late—report to him when chapel was over.

He made it very clear that they must never be late again. He spoke gently, but firmly. But his lecture wasn't really necessary. They knew when he called the meeting that they had displeased him, and had already resolved not to do that again.

They told each other how they had caught his spirit from special glimpses of him. Diana Schmuck recalled how he dealt with a discipline problem in the dorm.

"He didn't make a display of authority—he never needed to do that because no one wanted to hurt him. When this incident occurred he got the whole group together, sat them down and said, 'Now Sweethearts, we need to talk about this.'"

She remembered his helpfulness to the other teachers. They could always find him when they needed him. And often he seemed to know when they needed him, and would seek them out.

Diana, who had been comfortable as a camper, started on faculty after her junior year in college. She had been back one year, previously, as a faculty assistant, but it was hard for her to adjust to her new position.

As she walked from the Manor House to the Recital Hall, Wilmos came along, put his arm around her shoulder and asked, "How's it going? I want you to know I appreciate what you are doing." It was the encouragement she needed.

During that summer the mother of one of her students came to her in a rage. "My daughter should have been given one of the concert slots. She deserved an award!" she shouted. Diana did her best to explain, but the woman didn't want to listen.

Heartstrings

The encounter left Diana shaken and she went to Wilmos to tell him about it.

No one knows what he said to the student or to the mother, but when he finished with them he said to Diana, "Don't worry about it at all. I trust what you are doing. Put it behind you."

Diana, looking back on that, said, "I didn't know what an unusual thing that was for an administrator to do until I got out into the real world."

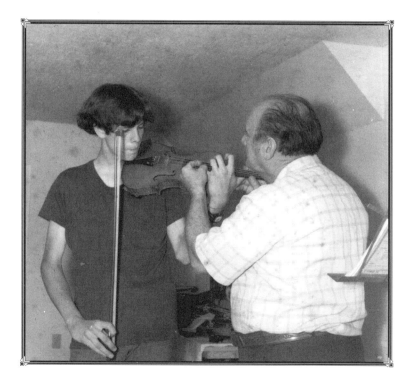

Teacher and student form a close relationship.

Heartstrings

Janet Rawleigh remembered how careful he was not to undermine her authority as an instructor. "He would come to orchestra rehearsal to help the students. He would never interrupt; he was more likely to just listen for problems so that he could work them out with the individual students during their private lessons."

He was a gift-giver, noticing people's special needs. That was how Lillian Pinkham remembered him. Her back trouble made it uncomfortable for her to sit on regular chairs. He made a special stool to fit her short legs, and, without saying a word, left it by her desk. Another time he left her a foot massager that he had made of wooden rollers.

Wilmos clowning around on a tricycle at a home where they stayed when on tour. 1958.

"He did unexpected things like that for everyone," Lillian said. "He just had a love for people—and a delightful sense of humor. He loved to play jokes on us."

For children, he often carried candy in his pocket, as his father had done, someone remembered.

"He never made a big thing of those morning walks when he prayed for his students," someone said.

"No," another added, "if anyone commented on his early rising, he would say he liked to listen to the weather report so he could pass it on to the campers at breakfast. But he always carried that list of students so he would not miss a single one in his prayers. And during the winter he often sent postcards saying, "Miss you...praying for you...""

"I know he really did miss them," Adi Cierpke confirmed. She said that Wilmos' life was so involved with the students during camp that when school was over, and the grounds were empty, he would become almost depressed. As he walked along the quiet paths he would kick stones out of the way in annoyance, and go off by himself to his studio.

Perhaps he went there to relive the days that had just ended—to remember each one of the campers and staff.

He liked to spend autumn evenings in the studio, with a fire in the stove, a bowl of popcorn, his golden retriever Candy snoozing nearby, and just one or two good friends for company, they recalled.

Heartstrings

He might work at repairing a violin, or make sketches as they talked.

At one time, roof repairs provided him with a pile of worn slates. The paintings he did on them were given as gifts, or sold—with the proceeds going right back into the school.

Wilmos was a man with a serious purpose, but there was another side to him that delighted in playing tricks on people—students or faculty. And he seemed to enjoy teasing his wife most of all. He would say to the audience, after Gladys had played the bells, "And now you know why I call her my Ding-a-Ling."

Jam sessions, natural when musician friends get together, continue after Wilmos is gone. Gladys Csehy at the piano, Alfred Hoffsommer on the right. Candy, the golden retriever, appears ready to act as emcee.

At one time, there were twins on the faculty. They were resigned to being called by the wrong name. It seemed no one could tell them apart. But Wilmos never mistook one for the other. They coaxed him to tell how he knew which was which. Finally, with an impish grin, he whispered to the young women, "I look at your legs!"

At a banquet where the trio was listed on the program, someone at the head table was struggling to pronounce Adi Cierpke's last name, and turned to Wilmos for help. He grinned, took a pen and quickly drew on the paper tablecloth something he had seen Adi's father sketch—a syrup jug and a key. "Just like that," he said, "syrup key!"

That section of tablecloth with his answer became a treasured souvenir.

He was a man in a hurry. He resented speed limits, but he obeyed them reluctantly. When someone pointed out to him one day that driving at slower speeds saved on gas, he grudgingly admitted there could be some benefit to driving at thirty-five miles per hour.

Normally the Csehys would eat dinner with the campers—unless it was pasta. If it was spaghetti on the menu, or lasagna, Wilmos would go back to their trailer and wait for Gladys to fix something he liked. No one could figure out when she had ever had the opportunity to learn to cook, but she would prepare beef or chicken for him, Hungarian style.

Heartstrings

While people saw the great respect Wilmos and Gladys showed for each other's musical ability, they did not know a lot about them as a couple, for they kept their personal lives private. If they had any disagreements, they did not air them in public. Nor did they make any public show of affection.

Perhaps because their private life was a sealed book, people took delight in noticing two little signals they would give each other in public.

There was a particular half-scowling look Wilmos would give Gladys if they were playing together and he was not entirely satisfied with her accompaniment. Only those who knew them well would notice it, or know what it meant.

On the other hand, if Wilmos made a statement from the platform that was not 100% accurate—mentioning a wrong date or town—Gladys would raise her index finger and tap the air. People would smile, knowing she was about to interrupt with the information he had forgotten. These corrections were accepted graciously.

Reminiscing now they thought that while both Gladys and Wilmos Csehy had been warm and outgoing toward their audiences and their students, they were quite different personalities, and those differences had made for a well-balanced team. Wilmos had been compassionate, caring deeply about individuals; a visionary, believing nothing was impossible with God.

Gladys was practical. With complete trust that God would provide all their needs, she had taken care of money matters, details of travel, student discipline, and made the daily routine of home and school run smoothly.

Staff members knew that Gladys kept a close watch on any money that was spent. They smiled, recalling a day when Wilmos had come into the office where she was working on the accounts. He said he was going to the mall and needed some money. Most reluctantly she put two dollars in the hand he was holding out.

He looked at it with amazement. "Well, thank you," he said. And left.

The people who had seen this little exchange burst out laughing, and teased Gladys about her generosity. When he came back, they asked him if he had spent it all in one place.

"I wanted to buy bullets to use on the rifle range," he explained. Then, with eyes twinkling, he admitted, "I charged them."

But people who had been with them in times of crises—doctors and nurses—remembered seeing the tenderness between them.

They seldom spoke of the long separations from their family when the children were small. It was something they believed had been required of them. But now someone quoted a remark Wilmos had made shortly before he died that indicated how hard it had been. "If I had to do it over, I'm not sure I would be strong enough to part with them."

As with their affection for each other, these were not emotions they had paraded in public.

They had enjoyed their grandchildren very much, and sometimes added to the time spent with them by hiring them to work at the camp.

Beyond their appreciation of Wilmos' personality, the school faculty, individually, had great respect for the musician that he was. They expressed this in different ways.

Wes White: "He was highly respected in the musical community for his mastery of classical music. When he chose to go into playing religious music—into an evangelistic ministry—he lost some of that proficiency as a classical player. He retained the ability; he had simply chosen something else. There was a passionate sound to his violin music."

Dr. Samuel Hsu: "I don't feel Wilmos was any less than the finest violinists. All the pianissimo sound, all the colors and effects that you hear in classical music were in his playing. Whether the hymn was about joy or about worship, the violin was obedient to him because of his skills. He was a lover of the violin. There was more in him, as in all great artists, than he could teach."

Adi Cierpke: "He did church hymns in a classical style. His music was soulful. He played and put his whole heart into it."

Diana Schmuck: "He was passionate in his playing and in his life."

Janet Rawleigh: "The outside world had great respect for Wilmos. They saw the classical foundation to his hymn arrangements."

Molly Fung: "His violin style had the flavor of his Hungarian background—almost folk music in that it was from the heart, very elaborate. He wanted to make the best sacred music. He really did that. I don't know anyone in that field today who can play the hymns like he could. He did it with more flair and spontaneity than you usually see."

*She is a brilliant pianist and plays
as he does—as the spirit directs.*
—Music Critic
Toronto Telegram

Chapter 11

Perhaps the thing that will be longest remembered about Wilmos Csehy is the absolute trust he had that God was in control and would never leave him in want.

"His prayers kept the school afloat," Dr. Sam Hsu has said.

In an interview during his last summer, Mr. Csehy said, "I don't think young people realize how real God is... Some of the kids ask how I dare to talk to the Lord like I do."

He went on to explain that at camp God answered prayer regularly. "My Father in heaven is rich. He has everything and so I have every right to come and ask Him. I have lived on that basis all these years…"

This was a faith that Gladys Csehy shared with her husband.

She marvels at the way God prepared their path, long before they knew where it would lead. Her own training is an example.

She had five years of piano lessons with a local teacher, starting when she was nine years old. When she later went to Taylor University as a mathematics major, she wanted to study with the head of the piano department there and arranged to take one lesson a week during her junior year.

"That teacher gave me one piece of sheet music for the whole year!" Gladys recounts. "It was about eleven pages. The rest of my lesson time was filled with scales, arpeggios, the dominant seventh, the diminished extension exercises, and that kind of thing.

"And exercises that would develop my hands and fingers to play relaxed and properly," she adds. "The one piece of sheet music she gave me was Liszt's arrangement of Schubert's 'Hark, Hark the Lark.' All the way through, the melody predominated, with an accompaniment rippling all over the piano."

In her senior year she increased her lessons to twice a week. "As I look back on it now, that teacher gave me, in her instruction, exactly what the Lord knew I was going to be needing down the road. It was perfect training for me to be an accompanist for fifty years and longer."

She had not yet met her future husband—an extraordinarily talented musician who had been raised by a man who could nurture that gift.

Again and again they would look back and see how God had been at work.

Wilmos wasn't timid about asking God for the necessities of life. But sometimes he was overwhelmed when God provided things he hesitated to ask for.

While he was living in New York in the 1940s, his violin studio was right next to Carnegie Hall. Nearby Luthier Rosenthal had a shop where he sold and repaired the very best violins. From this Latvian Jew, Wilmos learned how to repair violins.

People regularly brought instruments to his shop to be resold. Wilmos and his musician friends browsed through the stock regularly to see what new things had come in.

One day a particular violin caught his eye. *Carlo Ferdinando Landolfi*, the sign said. Landolfi violins were known for their wonderful tone—and for their high price tags. This one had been made in Milan, Italy, in 1772.

There in the shop he tried it out—and didn't want to put it down. It would be a dream come true to own such an instrument.

Wilmos was not the only one interested in it. Mischa Elman, who was twenty years older than he, looked at it with interest. Wilmos told him that it was a very fine violin.

"How do you know, until I play it?" Mr. Elman responded. He had been giving violin concerts since

Heartstrings

he was thirteen, and apparently didn't feel the need of anyone else's opinion.

The violin wasn't sold immediately. Each time Wilmos saw it; he wanted it even more. He learned that it had belonged to a man who had been in the U. S. Army. Serving in Italy with a division of flame-throwers, he had lost an arm, and could no longer draw music from the strings of a violin.

One day, one of his students came into the studio and thought Wilmos was unusually sober and quiet. "What's wrong?" he asked.

Wilmos said he had just been looking at a wonderful violin he would love to own, and the boy asked, "Is it so expensive? How much does it cost?"

When Wilmos told him $4,000, he responded, "Oh, that is a lot!"

Then, in 1937, it was more than a year's pay for the average man—if he even had a job. Three-bedroom houses were listed for sale at $2500.

After his lesson the boy went home, but within a few hours he telephoned his teacher and put his father on the phone. "I'd be glad to lend you the money to buy that Landolfi," the man told Wilmos.

"Oh, thank you, but I don't know that I would even be able to make payments on a loan like that."

"You don't need to be concerned about it. You just pay me whatever you can, whenever you can. If you can't pay it, we won't worry about it."

Following his benefactor's instructions, Wilmos went to meet him at a designated subway stop.

Heartstrings

Wilmos Csehy, 1937, purchasing a new violin, predecessor to the Landolfi he would acquire in the 1940's

Heartstrings

There he was handed a paper sack containing the entire amount of the loan in cash. Astonished, then terrified, he rode the subway back to the Bronx, sure that something would happen to the money before he got it safely home.

Wilmos was overjoyed at this generosity, and continued to be grateful each time he played the violin. Although he did repay most of the money, the man later made an outright gift of a part of the loan. In 1982 that instrument, purchased for $4,000, was appraised at $28,000.

Wilmos Csehy, trying out the new violin.

Copy of the certificate for the Landolfi violin.

It was not the only time God answered wishes for things Wilmos knew were not necessities. For their twenty-fifth wedding anniversary he wished he could replace the rather plain engagement ring he had given Gladys with something more valuable. But he wasn't in the habit of asking God for luxuries. Was this a luxury?

Heartstrings

Apparently not in God's eyes, for in a church where they were playing there was a jeweler...and Wilmos was able to give his wife a ring that more appropriately expressed his love for her.

Wilmos and Gladys Csehy with Mary Jane McCarty at the Csehy's 50th wedding anniversary celebration in 1983.

David Shockey said that Wilmos was a living example of the philosophy he so often quoted: "Pray as if everything depends on the Lord, and then work as if everything depends on you."

Long before the Csehy Summer School of Music had taken shape in their dreams, their travels all over the country made their name known in homes where there would someday be high school musicians looking for a summer camp.

Without even realizing it at the time, they were not only advertising a school that did not yet exist, but they were meeting people who would want to serve on the faculty and staff.

Equally important, they were making contacts with evangelists and Bible teachers. Although they had dreamed of someday having a school, they had never thought of directing a conference ground.

When the Csehys found themselves managing Muncy Terraces they had an impressive list of Bible teachers and evangelists among their friends. They were able to bring in well-known speakers such as Dr. Ralph Neighbor, Dr. Paul B. Smith, Rev. Woodrow Kroll, Dr. Wilbur Nelson, Rev. John DeBrine, Rev. David Virkler, Dr. Andrew Telford, and Russell Killman.

Their roster of speakers included A. W. Tozer, Richard Seume, Dr. Walter Wilson, Dr. Howard Sugden, Dr. Oswald J. Smith and his son Dr. Paul B. Smith, Dr. Lehman Strauss, Dr. Sidlow Baxter, Dr. R. G. Lee, Dr. Herbert Lockyer, and Dr. Dwight B. Pentecost.

Heartstrings

Dr. Joseph Stowell, Sr., pastor of Hackensack Baptist Church in the 1950's, and his son Joe who later became president of Moody Bible Institute, were close friends who would often drive to Flemington to fish with Wilmos and his father. They, too, came to speak at the Csehys' invitation.

"More of God's planning," Gladys explained. God had constantly been preparing ahead for needs they would have.

She remembered one day of crisis, when financial problems were at their worst and it seemed there was no way to save Muncy Terraces. Wilmos walked across the campus to a fateful meeting of the board members.

As he walked, he prayed, "God, if you want this place, take it. If you want us to have it, work it out." Those were not just words. He was ready for God's will.

At that meeting, someone offered the money that made it possible to keep going.

Gladys often stated that she didn't worry about anything. She trusted God completely to supply all of her needs.

In 1989 Lakeside Youth Services expressed an interest in Muncy Terraces. They took over the ownership of the property, and the papers that were finally signed gave both Gladys and Adi Cierpke lifetime rights to live on the property—terms that were renegotiated when the property later changed hands again.

Heartstrings

After Wilmos' death in 1983, Gladys served as director of Muncy Terraces for six years. When it came time to select a new administrator, she enthusiastically recommended Guy Kinney, an accomplished musician, conductor and teacher from Brooktondale New York. He was named executive director in 1991.

During his administration there came another evidence of God's providing for needs long before they occurred. Now in the position of being tenants at Muncy Terraces, the school's expenses began to exceed their income to the point that they needed to consider other locations. Through the years a strong relationship had developed between the Csehy School and Philadelphia College of Bible. Many PCB instructors spent their summers teaching at Csehy. Both schools shared the goal of developing the talents in young people who would use their gifts to honor the Lord. It seemed that God had been at work knitting these two schools together for a long time.

When Lakeside announced that they were selling the property that had been home to the summer school for twenty-seven years, Philadelphia College of Bible invited the Csehy School of Music to use their campus in Langhorne, Pennsylvania.

With thanksgiving for God's provision, Csehy moved its best pianos into the music department at PCB, and held classes at its new quarters in the summer of 1995.

Heartstrings

In a sense, it was the end of an era when Gladys Csehy moved on to her heavenly home on June 22, 2001.

The school she and Wilmos started was gearing up for its 40th year. Leadership had passed to Randy Haynes. PCB, the school's home, had a new name, Philadelphia Biblical University.

But the goals for the Csehy Summer School of Music did not change.

Wilmos Csehy's dream of teaching teenagers the beauty of good music and the joy of walking with God has been realized many times over.

The school's dedicated directors and faculty have caught the Csehys' vision and are determined to keep the dream and the reality alive.

Heartstrings

Wilmos Csehy onstage at the Csehy Summer
School of Music in Muncy Pennsylvania.
(Photograph by Dr. Gordon Bobbett.)

Heartstrings

Philadelphia Biblical University
The Csehy School's home since 1995

Heartstrings

Csehy; The Future

A Message from the Director

The goals of the Csehy Summer School of Music remain the same—to see young musicians learn to love classical music and perform it at an advanced level; to see those same young people lovingly taught by committed Christians.

However, change is inevitable. To ignore changing times and methods is to invite failure. Though the message of Csehy will remain the same, increased use will be made of the Internet to recruit students and publicize the school.

We will continue the tradition of weekly student concerts—open to the public. Our website now offers samples of these concerts. Csehy has long been an international program. The Internet expands our communication possibilities with prospective students in distant countries.

The number of homeschooling families is exploding. Some may be able to provide private music lessons for their children, but be unable to find ensemble opportunities for them. Csehy Summer School of Music will fill that void.

Since the move to the Philadelphia area in 1995, there has been an ever-growing number of inquiries from families who want the Csehy experience for their children, but lack the financial means to make it happen. The school, working primarily through alumni, will increase the financial aid for these inner city and underprivileged youngsters.

As the world rushes headlong away from all that is decent, holy and reverent, Csehy knows it is critical to hold the line and uphold the musical and spiritual standards that motivated Wilmos and Gladys Csehy. As the gap grows between what young people hear from the world and what they hear at Csehy, the school will continue to provide a place for reflection and introspection, giving young musicians the opportunity to discover what Wilmos so desperately wanted them to know: Music is a gift from the God of the Universe and is to be used for His honor and His glory. Our musical and spiritual standards—Wilmos Csehy's legacy—will, by God's grace and by His might, be like Christ himself, "…the same yesterday, today and forever."

    Randy Haynes, Director
    The Csehy Summer School of Music
    June 2004

Visit **www.csehy.com** to learn more about the Csehy Summer School of Music.

The Ceshy Summer School of Music
P.O. Box 1004
Langhorne, PA 19047
(215) 702-4407

Csehy Musical Memories CD
Produced by
The Csehy Summer School of Music

Music crossed the boundary lines of Hungary, Prussia, and the United States to bring together three gifted artists, uniting their talents to produce an excellent musical treat.

Hear the beautiful music of Wilmos Csehy (performing on the rare Carlos Ferdinando Landolfi violin), Gladys Csehy, (accompanying on the piano), lyric soprano Adi Cierpke and other team members from early ministry days. The brilliant arrangements blend the violin, piano, vibraharp and chimes in recordings made between 1950 and 1965 by the Csehy Musical Messengers.

Csehy Musical Memories CD, Vol. 1

For more information:
The Csehy Summer School of Music
P.O. Box 1004
Langhorne, PA 19047
(215) 702-4407
www.csehy.org

If you wish to order or to find out more information about:

Heartstrings
A Biography of Wilmos Csehy
by Barbara M. Sutryn
ISBN 1-892135-33-7

or

Csehy Musical Memories CD

Please contact:

Lamp Post Publishing, Inc.
1741 Tallman Hollow Road,
Montoursville, PA 17754
800-326-9273
(570) 435-2804
Fax (570) 435-2803
www.HeartstringsBio.com